Career Detection
Finding and Managing Your Career

Brian McIvor

How to use this book

Finding and managing your career can be a bit of a mystery!
This book can be used in two ways:

❶ If you are completely unsure of what you want out of your career work through all of the exercises in Chapters 1-7, complete the Career Blueprint at the end of the book and use the goal setting tools in Chapter 10 to plan your next moves. If you do not wish to write on the text there is a PDF workbook available for free on-line at *www.brianmcivor.com*. Chapters 8 and 9 are additional resources to help you deal with common problems

❷ If you are clear about most of your career issues consult the book plan that is evident within the Table of Contents to check what you need. It is suggested that you use the Career Blueprint to double-check that you have everything!

© 2008 Brian McIvor
ISBN 0-9519738-5-1
ISBN 978-0-9519738-5-1

All design, art work and liaison with printers has been undertaken by
Neworld Associates, 9 Greenmount Avenue, Harold's Cross, Dublin 12. www.neworld.com

Publisher: Managements Briefs, 30 The Palms, Clonskeagh, Dublin 14.

Preface

My mind loves to play 'word association'. As I was thinking about this book by my dear friend, the other day, the following went through my mind

→ **The Sky** is: Blue, cloudy, gorgeous, sunny, threatening, stormy, majestic, foretelling heaven

→ **Life** is: Sweet, earnest, unpredictable, problematic, poetic, puzzling, magnificent, invigorating, a great gift, to be savoured

→ **Career planning** is: Optional, mandatory, helpful, enlightening, intelligent, detailed, life-saving, life-changing

→ *Brian McIvor* is: Gifted, brilliant, inventive, helpful, caring, musical, creative, determined, humble, persistent, faithful, life-changing, loyal, a born teacher, a friend of great price.

And **You** are: Lucky, lucky, lucky, to have this friend, and to have this book, to guide you through career planning, that you might enjoy a better life and live triumphantly, under skies sunny or stormy.

I am the author of a book called *What Color Is Your Parachute? A Practical Manual for Job-Hunters and Career-Changers* (revised annually, 10 million copies in print.) I first met the author many years ago, when he showed up at one of my annual workshops in the U.S. He impressed us all with his intellect, sweetness of character, creativity, driving anxiousness to be helpful, and lousy sense of humour. (He told the most awful jokes. They have improved, over the years.) One of my annual staff, who had been with me for many, many years, now looking for a chance to retire, came up to me one day, and said, "I think I've just met my successor." And so he had.

The next year, Brian joined my annual staff, and for several years came over to the U.S. (or from your point of view, went over to the U.S.) every summer, where he contributed brilliantly to each workshop. He became virtually indispensable.

He went back to Ireland, determined to share what he had learned — not only from me but from many whom he first met at my workshops:

Daniel Porot, Jim Kell, John Lees, John Webb, Pete Hawkins, and Chuck Young, to name but a few. He wanted not merely to share these people's ideas with all of Ireland, but to conduct a virtual crusade, to carry career planning to every nook and cranny of his beloved country. And to the mix he has added many, many original ideas of his own, such as that of 'the career detective,' that you will find in this book. He is now the pre-eminent expert on career planning in your whole country. Radio, television, newspapers, and workshops have made his name, and his gentle determined crusade, known everywhere.

I am so glad he has put together this book, this workbook, for I know it will help everyone who reads it, and does it, and applies it to his or her own life. You have a truly gifted man in your midst, one of the kind that Ireland has always been famous for. He is more than just a gifted teacher. He has been a constant, helpful, devoted friend to me over all these years, and with this workbook, you will find him now to be an immensely helpful friend to you.

Dick Bolles
Author, *"What Color is Your Parachute?"*

Table of Contents

Acknowledgements

This book is dedicated to those who have helped, supported and encouraged me over the years in the pursuit of the great Career Mystery: Pat, my wife, my parents and family, my former colleagues in the Civil Service, the Institute of Public Administration, the Irish Management Institute, Irish Life and Permanent, The *What Color is Your Parachute* International Career Workshops Faculty and, more recently, the Retirement Planning Council of Ireland.

In the field of Career development I was greatly influenced by Richard Nelson Bolles, Author of *What Color is Your Parachute?* Many of the ideas in this book arose out of my involvement with his International Workshops over the years and my debt to him is considerable. Other major influences were Daniel Porot, author of the PIE Career Method and Dr. Peter Hawkins of Liverpool University author of the Windmills Project and of the WLPG process described in Chapter 5. Thank you, Pete for reading the manuscript and offering so many useful suggestions.

Special thanks also to *Lucinda Bray, Carol Christen, Eamon Donnelly, Mary Hanson, Jim Kell, Gráinne Killeen, Louise Karch, John Lees, Ciarán McGettrick, Jack Morrissey, Kevin O'Kelly, John Webb,* and *Chuck Young* for their help and encouragement.

Brian McIvor

December 2008

Introduction

"Be your own career detective because it would take a Sherlock Holmes to show you how to find and manage your career."

International surveys show consistently that more than one in two job-holders are in the wrong job – but choose to do nothing about it. Longer hours and increased levels of stress play an increasing part of a professional career than 10 years ago. But there is a downside; a recent UK survey suggests that about one in six employees have seriously considered sabotaging the company they work for. So a lot of discontent in the workplace – but how did it happen and what can be done? Most people spend more time planning their annual holiday than planning their career. When jobs are plentiful people drift to the most accessible ones; in a recession they take what they can get. What's missing in either case is a process to match your job with your skills, your expertise, your way of working so that you can have a career and not just a job.

To do this you have to be your own career detective – ferreting out hard-to-get information, making contacts and ultimately making sense of a lot of data. Most people need help with this; when we do this for ourselves we can run into self-doubt or over-confidence. I became interested in the notion of the career detective from a chance remark made by a colleague. He said that "job seeking is like being your own detective agency". The more I thought about my favourite detective stories the more the plots resembled the process of finding a career – plenty of mystery and ambiguity, some red herrings and lot of diversion and, finally, a reconciliation of all the strands in an elegant solution.

To put things into perspective - we need to work like detectives using the following:

→ **The forensics:** Ability and personality tests to get some objectivity into the process

→ **Our skills:** To work with people, information and things to find our dream career

→ **Our knowledge:** We all have acquired various forms of expertise in our life that potentially can be of use to us

→ **Witness statements:** Feedback from our friends, colleagues, peers and mentors, to find out what your skills are, you need to examine what you have done

→ **Intuition and Logic:** The ability to deal with our situation logically and systematically and, at the same time, to be creative in seeing opportunities where others may see problems

→ **A network:** Contacts who can make things easier for us – and who we can help in return. It also means staying clear of people who are cynical, toxic or just plain unhelpful

→ **Persistence:** Many give up the job of working on their career plan because of apathy, or just get discouraged. A good detective doesn't let the case go because nobody can see a solution- to succeed you need good information, good logic and a bit of good luck

→ **Goals:** To be clear what you want and what you don't want; to be able to distinguish between wants and needs and to set goals that are right for you

WHY do I need a career plan?

1

Chapter 1 outline
WHAT is my career?

→   What am I looking for?
→   What will the rewards be for me?
→   12 challenges to your career in the
     21st Century
→   10 questions you should ask yourself
     about your career
→   What are you looking for?
     A career or a job?
→   What is success?
→   Values, goals and legacy
→   What anchors your career choices?
→   Elements of the Career Process
→   Your own personal success statement

Introduction

A career could be defined as a plan or blueprint of your working life.

To have a successful career means that the right things happen at the right time and that you move upwards to achieve your potential. If something unforeseen happens you will need a plan to put you back on course — or change to a better one. Each career plan is unique and this book offers a blueprint which will include the successful elements of your career.

What am I looking for?

A job? A career? A particular lifestyle?
It's your decision.

This chapter will help you set your sights on a career. You will need a job that will do more than just pay the bills.

Is a career plan really necessary? YES! Because:

1 There will be constant changes in your work, life style and environment until the day you retire or die

2 In the 21st Century managing your career will be something that will need to be done by you and nobody else

3 You will be judged on job performance and delivery of objectives— if you are in the right job for yourself it will be easier to meet demanding objectives. If you are not — you may suffer stress and burnout

4 Your standard of living and security of employment may suffer unless you actively manage your career

5 Your life outside work may suffer unless you manage the boundaries between work and the rest of your life.

What will the rewards be for me?

→ Your work will match your capacity to do it

→ You will be more likely to be paid what you are really worth

→ You will find the job and the work that is right for you rather than taking the first thing that comes

→ You will be better equipped to deal with change in the workplace

→ You will be recognised as being proactive, engaged, successful — and unique!

12 challenges to your career in the 21st Century

Your personal challenge is to manage your career under the following conditions:

1 **Disappearance of the "Job for Life":** 21st century organizations tend to hire on a contract basis for as long as the bottom line holds

2 **Changing organisations mean changing jobs:** Mergers, acquisitions and redeployment mean organisation structures keep changing; new technologies and processes mean that no job description stays constant. You may find that you will change careers (not just jobs!) up to **eight** times during your life

3 **Longer working hours and lack of boundaries:** Although there are directives on maximum working hours many people in corporate life do not know when to call stop and enjoy their leisure without guilt

4 **Higher incidences of stress in the workplace:** Including the effects of increased levels of commuting

5 **Effects of technology:** Rapid changes in technology mean that you may become de-skilled very quickly unless you constantly re-train

6 **Working from home:** Now a standard feature of life for many in Information-technology businesses

7 **Economic Prosperity:** Higher standards of living

8 **Threats:** Security and Terrorism

9 **Globalisation:** Your job may be outsourced to another part of the world at very short notice

10 **"Right Fit":** Ensuring that the job you are in is right for you: 1 in 2 employees feel they are in the wrong job -but most choose to do nothing about it

11 **Lifestyle:** One of the consequences of a period of prosperity has been the emphasis on picking a lifestyle that combines the non-work elements: Family, social contacts and recreation

12 **Commuting:** Commuting times are getting longer, roads are more congested, public transport is inadequate, homes are increasingly further away from places of work and the oil could **run out...**

10 questions you should ask yourself about your career

If you answer less than eight with a yes do you have a career problem?

1 You travel to your job with eager expectation most mornings of your life ☐

2 You feel that your job is one that interests you and engages you ☐

3 Your job has helped develop your skills ☐

4 Your job has helped you develop your confidence and self esteem ☐

5 Working conditions for you are ideal ☐

6 Relationships at work with colleagues, customers and superiors are optimum ☐

7 You get regular and constructive feedback from your superiors ☐

8 Your work receives the recognition it truly deserves ☐

9 At the end of the day you are truly thankful for your chosen career ☐

10 Your workplace is a really enjoyable place to be ☐

What are you looking for? A career or a job? What's the difference?

A Job...	A Career...
→ Is something you do for money	→ Is something you do to fulfil your potential
→ Has a job description	→ Is part of your life plan
→ Has content decided by others	→ Is managed by you
→ Can lead to burn out	→ Leads to fulfilment
→ Has to be justified constantly	→ Has to be reviewed constantly
→ Can be terminated at a moment's notice	→ Is for life (if you choose)
→ Is connected to the organisation's goals and bottom line	→ Is part of your life goals
→ Is focussed on results	→ Is focussed on values

In this chapter we shall consider career in terms of the job, the rewards, your value system and – ultimately the legacy you want to leave. In Chapter 2 we shall look at career in terms of work and life balance.

What is success?

What's your personal definition of success?

Think of what it would be like to have a successful career:

→ What would the rewards be?

→ What would your lifestyle be?

→ How would it feel?

Activity 1: *What's the definition of success you have been carrying around for the last few years?*

Success definition 1:
Current definition of success in one sentence: First thoughts.

> **Why do I need this?**
> **Your definition of success may be out of date!**

Most definitions of success will contain elements of the following:

What you earn, the type of house you live in, where you will go on your holidays, your favourite possessions and the fun things you will do. Think again! Reflect on what is **really** valuable in your life: *Your relationships, your experiences.*

Think of defining success in terms of breadth and depth. There are two major ways of defining success one of which could be frustrating:

❶ Success = **Having** then **Doing** and then **Being**

"When I win the Lottery I shall have what I want and be able to do what I want and then I will be who I need to be."

This approach starts with confusing 'wants' with 'needs' and goes downhill from there.

❷ Success = **Being** then **Doing** and then **Having**

"When I understand who I am (to be) then I shall know what to do and I shall have what I want"

This approach starts with identifying your needs, aspirations, skills and talents; you are then in an ideal position to work toward your goals confident in the knowledge that you are looking for what you really need. In this way you will find your best energy.

HAVE, DO, BE versus BE, DO, HAVE: WHAT's the DIFFERENCE?

Defining SUCCESS as focussing first on HAVING , then DOING and then BEING means:

→ You are guided by other peoples' definitions of success

→ Your focus is on the externals - such as money or status

→ Your thinking may be dominated by constant comparison with others and considering yourself a failure because you are not as rich as X or Y

→ You are guided by conventional career routes

→ There is no place in the plan for failure; every step must be a successful one

→ What other people think is more important than what you yourself *really* think

→ Ultimately success is elusive because somebody else out there is more successful than you

→ You end up being frustrated

Defining SUCCESS as a focus on BEING, then DOING and then HAVING means:

→ Your focus is internal and on who you really are instead of who other people want you to be

→ You concentrate on the things you that you are passionate about

→ Understanding the best you can achieve - in a realistic and grounded way

→ There are as many different career paths as there are people; you find the back doors as well as the front doors

→ What you need to DO follows logically — because it is right for you

→ The reward (the HAVING) follows logically

→ FAILURE and SIDETRACKING are allowed. Your maxim becomes "there is no failure — only learning"

→ You value your own past experience and learning

→ You end up following a path that is right for you

Examining success from as many angles as possible will allow you to establish a more realistic career and life path for yourself — and allow you the opportunity to separate wants from needs.

Activity 2:
IDENTIFYING CAREER SUCCESS, BE, DO, HAVE

Consider these questions

→ *What would I like to BE?*

→ *What would I like to DO?*

→ *What do I want to HAVE?*

Fill out the table below initially work from left to right:

→ E.g. If I wanted to **be** (happy, secure) what would that be like?

→ What would I be **doing**? (e.g. *be in the right job?*)

→ And what would I **have** after that? (*The right salary, the right lifestyle*)

Be	Do	Have

Why do I need this? **Success is a complex concept and we each have our own version of it. Elements of success are linked and some have priority over others**

VALUES, GOALS and LEGACY

Values are the principles by which you act every day, in your job, in your life work, with your friends and relations. Your values permeate everything that you do and your life should be a reflection of them. In your chosen career, you should be working in a place where the value system is in harmony with your own. This is not to imply that all of your values should be expressed through your work, but there should be an area of common overlap.

Here are some samples:

→ **Justice and Fair Play**: Ensuring that everybody's rights are respected in the workplace and elsewhere

→ **Inclusion**: Making sure that the circles you move in are not exclusive or limiting

→ **Service to the community:** Consider the various communities you belong to

→ **Excellence**: Striving for the best in everything that you do

→ **Empathy:** Sensitivity to the feelings, needs, wants and desires of others

→ **Goals:** What you want to achieve as the expression of your values.

Personal goals are relatively easily quantified and realised. Some life goals are in themselves unattainable – for example to live completely without stress or conflict.

Identifying your legacy:

→ What do you want to do to make the world a better place for your being there?

→ How do you want to contribute to the welfare of the world?

→ What would you like your imprint on the planet to be?

Activity 3:
Complete this statement:

I want to leave the world having contributed the following: -

Why do I need this?
To get a your career into perspective.

We shall return to this idea at the end of the chapter.

What anchors your career choices?

Your career is anchored by your career drivers. Drivers are inner forces that guide your choice in work and outside it e.g. some people look for a career that gives them meaningful work which is useful to others; others look for a career that gives them money or power.

What are you looking for?

Activity 4:

Here's a simple way to find your career drivers:

Rank the following from 1 to 9 in terms of what is really important to you in your career

RANKING:
From 1= This is the most important thing to me in my career.
To 9= This is the least important thing to me in my career
Constantly ask the question: What's *really* important to me in my career and in my life? If you do not identify your career drivers correctly you may follow the wrong career for the wrong reasons! Take time to reflect on what you *need,* rather than what you *want!*

Ranking

Ranking	Driver
9	**MONEY and POSSESSIONS** I crave a very high standard of living
5	**POWER and INFLUENCE** I want to be in control of people and resources
2	**MEANING** I want my career to involve things which I believe to be valuable for their own sake
8	**EXPERTISE** I want to achieve a high level of accomplishment in a specialised field
7	**CREATIVITY** I would like to innovate and to be identified with original output
3	**AFFILIATION** I want to have fulfilling relationships with others at work
6	**AUTONOMY** I want to be independent and able to make key decisions for oneself
4	**SECURITY** I want a solid and predictable future
1	**STATUS** I want to be recognised, admired and respected by the world at large

Your top three drivers:

1	2	3

The Career Equation

Your Ideal Career = Your Ideal ROLE + Your Ideal FIELD of activity.

In your ideal career you need to be doing the right thing in the right place

→ **Your ideal ROLE**
Identified by focussing on what you favourite and best transferable skills are; this will be the subject of Chapter 3

→ **Your ideal FIELD of activity**
Identified by focussing on what you know and are enthusiastic about, examining what you have learned formally or informally and finding the fields or industries that value that knowledge; this will be the subject of Chapter 5

The main idea is to maximise the things that you are best at and enjoy and find the places where they are valued.

The main questions are:

→ Am I in the right ROLE?

→ Am I in the right FIELD?

→ Which of these needs to be changed, abandoned, overhauled or left as is?

Elements of the Career Process

Career planning is a cyclical process which will involve keeping the following main elements under constant review.

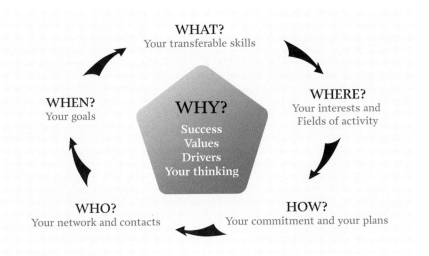

Before planning, moving to or moving from your current career or role you need to have the following elements identified:

→ **Find the Reasons:**
The WHY: This will involve understanding yourself, your ideas of success, your ideal work and life balance and the reasons why your situation is different from others'. Covered in this chapter and Chapter 2

→ **Your Transferable Skills:**
The WHAT: To identify your core skills you have built up over your life and career to date and to identify any skills gaps you may have to close in moving forward. This also means taking a look at what you have done to date in your life and work and taking stock of yourself – to be covered in Chapter 3

→ **Your Interests and the Fields of Activity they can be applied to:**
The WHERE: To identify the location, the type of organisation, outcomes, salary, and people you want to work for. Marry the WHAT and the WHERE to your Research about your target field(s) to get the job or career move you want. To be covered in Chapters 4 and 5

→ **Identify How you will work:**
The HOW: What strategies will you use? You will need to Commit yourself to the process, Plan in the short and long term and Review constantly. Develop your own strategies. Use Informational Interviewing to Collect data for **Pleasure**, for **Information** and for **Employment.** You will also need a **Plan B.** *To be covered in Chapter 6*

→ **Identify your network:**
The WHO: The people who will be your eyes and ears re information, opportunities and jobs. The network will be something you will put time into – to support others in their journey. *To be covered in Chapter 7*

→ **Identify the Time Scale:**
The WHEN: Get used to setting goals and taking small risks. **Set Goals**: That are **SMART**: Specific, Measurable, Achievable, Relevant to your agenda and not to others and Time-bound. *To be covered in Chapter 10*

Your own personal success statement.

Activity 5:
Reflect on the points above and have another go at your success statement – considering both your career and your life.

Success definition 2:
After further consideration: Include who you want to be, what you want to do in your career, in your life outside work, what you would like to have and the legacy you will leave:

WHY? In my career I would like

Why do I need this?
To get a your career into perspective. To have a headline to aim for.

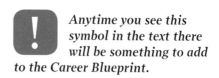

When you have finished this exercise you can copy the information into the WHY box on the Career Blueprint at the back of the book. We recommend that you copy the sheet and magnify to A3 size for better results.

Anytime you see this symbol in the text there will be something to add to the Career Blueprint.

Congratulations! You have completed the first piece of the solution to your career mystery.

Chapter 1 Summary

To find out what you want and what you are really looking for as a career detective will deal with the following challenges:

→ Establishing a career plan that suits you but which will be reviewed regularly — you may have up to eight (8!) career changes between first job and retirement

→ Defining what success is for you: What you want, what you really need and the legacy you want to leave

→ Deciding whether you want a career (which can lead to success and fulfilment) or just a job (which can lead to stress and burnout)

→ Understanding your career anchors — which vary from individual to individual

→ Combining of your ideal **role** in your ideal **field** of activity; to find these out you must know your favourite skills and expertise

→ Asking six major questions constantly:

1 **WHY?** — To make sure you are on the right track

2 **WHAT?** — To establish what your skills and expertise are

3 **WHERE** — To identify a place where you can work effectively, be recognised and rewarded

4 **HOW?** — To check your attitude and commitment

5 **WHO?** — To identify the people who can help you in your search; and

6 **WHEN?** — To set your goals — so that you can achieve real results quickly

ACTION PLANNING:
Nothing happens without a commitment to action!

Activity 6:
List some specific actions to make this happen:

	Action	Date	Desired outcome
1			
2			
3			

Example:

	Action	Date	Desired outcome
1	Study for MBA business degree	2012 (Qualify)	Deeper understanding of how a business works so I become more promotable
2			
3			

Are my Work and Life in Balance?

2

Chapter 2 outline
Getting Work and Life in Balance

→   Balancing sustainability and vision

→   The four components of Career and Life
    Balance: *Working, Learning, Playing*
    and *Giving*

→   Getting life into proportion

→   Stress and burnout

→   Knowing yourself – personality tests
    and profiles

→   Examining your role models

Introduction

For your career to be successful the proportion of the time you spend at work needs to allow sufficient time for the other elements. This chapter identifies the priority items and how they work in relation to each other.

Balancing Sustainability and Vision

In managing your career there are two elements which have to be taken into account and kept in balance during the process:

❶ **Sustainability**
This means ensuring that your skills sets and expertise are up-to-date and marketable. It also means that you have to ensure an income stream to cover commitments. To maximise your sustainability you will need to know what the market is looking for and what you have to offer

❷ **Vision**
This involves identifying what you want (see Chapter 1 on success) and what you are capable of. Your vision is based on what you are passionate about and what enthuses you

The great balancing act: Balancing sustainability and career vision

→ **Sustainability without vision**
Means that you follow the "hot careers" in the market place and follow the money. Going this route exclusively means that you will be driven purely by what pays but not by what you are interested in

Ultimately, you can wind up in a job that will pay well but means nothing. Worse still, you may burn out as you become one of those "indispensables" who enjoys a well-paid job which means nothing. Without vision you will have no aspirations and ultimately no satisfaction

→ **Vision without sustainability**
Means that you follow your dream — whether or not it is connected to reality. You may end up doing what you enjoy but the financial rewards may be too low to give you any real enjoyment of life. The things that are part of your vision may not be marketable and may have to be abandoned or side-lined while you make ends meet. Your choice is then whether your vision becomes your hobby

→ **Combining vision and sustainability**
What you ideally need to do is combine both. At the start of our careers we are low on both vision and sustainability. We may lack the vision if we have followed the herd at school and went where there were opportunities rather than asking ourselves what we **really** needed. In time we can explore our vision by study, by taking part-time work, volunteer work or attachments

Your career path?

From low sustainability and low vision to high sustainability and high vision.

As you add knowledge of your skills and expertise your sustainability will grow as well as your vision. It would be useful to try and get feedback and coaching to help you maximise your vision and profile. The diagram below shows your options. As you start the process you have both low vision and low sustainability. Low self-esteem may not help either. Your ultimate goal is the career that has both vision and sustainability maximised. To maximise your vision you may need a better sense of what you are capable of. Information

interviewing and networking which we cover in later chapters are powerful ways of bringing the vision forward. Continual goal setting and review will also help bring you forward.

Career Paths

Your objective is to get to a position of maximum sustainability and vision as quickly as possible. If you are lucky enough to be on a career fast track this will happen automatically. However, if the order of the day is to change your career path every few years your career path may resemble the dotted line in the graphic above. If a boom economy turns into a recessionary one you may have no choice but to follow the money and go down the sustainability route.

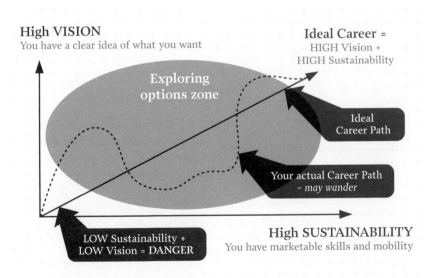

High VISION
You have a clear idea of what you want

Exploring options zone

Ideal Career =
HIGH Vision +
HIGH Sustainability

Ideal Career Path

Your actual Career Path
- *may wander*

LOW Sustainability + LOW Vision = DANGER

High SUSTAINABILITY
You have marketable skills and mobility

Activity 1: *Identifying my vision and sustainability*

Elements of my Career Vision	What makes me sustainable in a 21st century marketplace?
1	
2	
3	
4	

e.g. "to be at the top of my profession" "to be an empowering leader."

e.g. "having language skills in a global marketplace"

The four components of Career and Life Balance: *Working, Learning, Playing* and *Giving*

① Working

→ What is your life's work? It includes not only your job but other outside work; this is where you should combine your best skills, knowledge and traits to achieve satisfying results. Your objective here is to make your job into your career by doing things that you enjoy, that you have a flair for and for which somebody will pay you. In terms of maintaining balance in your life your objective here is ensure that your working week has limits to it – and that you do not take your work home – unless you **really** have to

② Learning

→ You need learning not only on the job but in other areas of your life. Your task here is to revise current levels of skills, acquire new knowledge, deal with change, manage your stress, and cope with the increasingly complex environment and grow in your own wisdom and learning

❸ Playing

→ How much time do you spend at sports, pastimes, amusement and just plain fun?

→ How do you recreate yourself and keep your body and mind active? One of the best stress-busting techniques is to have activities outside work where you do not have to think of work

→ Are you playful in your approach to the other three elements: Working, Learning and Giving? If not you may be missing the joy in your life!

❹ Giving

→ Think of the people in your life who you support and who, in turn, support you

→ Itemise your relationships: - Family, friends, community and the world at large; and your role in helping them meet **their** special needs through your special gifts. Up to point of retirement approximately 80% of our social contacts during the years of work are at work with colleagues

In a balanced lifestyle all of these may overlap. For example, if you work in the right job learning will be essential, interesting and welcome. Incorporating elements of play into your learning may even produce better results in less time.

However, there is no unique formula that works for everybody. People differ in the extent to

Incorporating elements of play into your learning may even produce better results in less time

which their world at work overlaps the world outside. For some, all four elements combine on the job — the working, the learning, the play and the giving. For others, play may be something to be done outside work with other people. Questions of privacy, others' needs and personal style may need to be taken into consideration in arriving at the right balance.

❶ How do you allocate your time between the four elements of working, learning, playing and giving?

❷ How do they overlap? How much is learning part of what you do at work?

❸ Are you adding new skills and expertise to your repertoire? If you don't you will become less employable

23

Getting Life into Proportion

Activity 2
Draw a diagram of the four elements:
Working, Learning, Playing, and Giving.

Step 1
Draw four circles in proportion to the amount of time they occupy in your life.

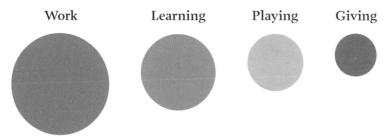

Step 2
Draw the diagram showing how they overlap.

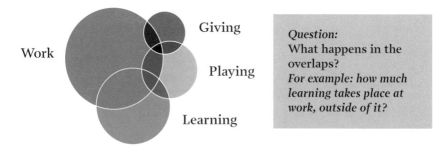

Question:
What happens in the overlaps?
For example: how much learning takes place at work, outside of it?

Why do I need this?
To identify the elements of your life and work in proportion.

Examine where elements of your WLPG overlap: *Example*

Overlap	What happens here
→ Working and Learning → Playing and giving	→ On-the-job mentoring of my staff → Coaching the local football team

Step 3
Draw the diagram the way you would like your life balance to be.
Is it the same as in Step 2 opposite?

Why do I need this?
To create the vision of your future career and life in balance.

Activity 3
In moving forward which items will remain constant and which will change?

Analyse the two diagrams:

What will remain the same?	What will need to change?
1	**1**
2	**2**
3 etc	**3 etc**

If you're stuck here are some examples:

What will remain the same?	What will need to change?
1 Family	**1** Associates
2 Core skills	**2** Work that doesn't suit me
3 etc	**3 etc**

Why do I need this?
1. To identify the constants in your life.
2. To reassure you about the things that can remain the same!

Stress and burnout

Stress and lifestyle are two major killers in the 21st century and the typical workplace can be stressful at the best of times. Over two thirds of all visits to doctors in western society relate to stress related illness. You have an obligation to manage your own stress. Your stress levels can be adversely affected by being in the wrong job. Stress can turn to strain and then you become physically or emotionally ill. Stress can arise because of a conflict between the demands placed on us and our resources to deal with them. A classic

> **Stress can arise because of a conflict between the demands placed on us and our resources to deal with them.**

stressor is being in the wrong job for poor pay, doing work you don't like — *often badly* getting negative performance reviews from your manager. Such a situation may feel so desperate that there is no hope of escape. Becoming aware of how bad things are and deciding to move on is a very empowering decision.

Consider the following strategies for dealing with stress

❶ **Physical exercise;** Walking, swimming and cycling are probably the best. Physical release is the centre of most successful strategies

❷ **Sharing your problems with a family member or a very close friend.** Before you go for therapy consider some form of peer counselling or sharing where you can support others and be supported in turn; this is preferable to surrendering your power unnecessarily to a therapist. Beware, however of inappropriate disclosure to those who will not treat the information with discretion or respect. Sharing (and solving) problems on a regular basis in the right place prevents inappropriate reactions in the workplace

❸ **Humour.** Laughing releases chemicals in the mind which change our brain state. It's said that when we laugh we learn quickest

❹ **Meditation and reflection.** Get into a space where you can just become present to yourself. Find space where you can have un-disturbed time. In the workplace find ways of composing yourself before the day starts and, if possible, for reviewing progress at the end of the day

Activity 4
List your personal stress busters:

Physical	Emotional	Spiritual

Why do I need this?
There many different strategies for dealing with stress – the gym is not the only option. You may already have other very effective stress strategies in place in your life already.

Activity 5
Moving Forward

Identify the things that will help you realise your vision of a balanced life. Identify the things that will get in your way. Which of these

1 Are you in control of? (e.g. your attitude)
2 Can you influence? – Even partially (e.g. friends, colleagues)
3 Can you only be concerned about? (e.g. the economy, global warming)

Here is a sample of what you can do:

	Under my control	I can influence these items	I can only be concerned about these
Will help me move forward	→ Attitude → Re-education	→ Identifying possible employers → Family → Friends	→ Boom economy on the way
Will Stop me moving forward	→ Lack of confidence → Not planning → Money	→ Prophets of doom	→ Worldwide recession on the way → Global warming

> *Why do I need this?*
> To show the difference between the things you can change and the things you need to leave alone!

Fill out the following table for yourself :

	Under my control (1)	I can influence these items (2)	I can only be concerned about these (3)
Will help me move forward ('GO' Items)			
Will Stop me moving forward ('STOP' Items)			

Examine both lists: *Where does the balance of power lie?*

Mark where you think it lies on the line below:

▶‖‖‖◀

All systems GO   *STOP and GO Equal*   *All Systems STOP*

Knowing yourself: *Personality tests and profiles*

One of the most powerful resources available to the career changer is some instrument or questionnaire that gives your data about yourself. Any psychometric tests must be viewed properly in context. A competent practitioner will let you know what the tests actually establish and will be equally clear as to what they don't establish. As with forensic evidence, psychometric tests operate out of probability. The object of many psychometric tests is to tell where you are in a typical population with regard to a particular skill or trait. It is up to you to use that information and to put it properly in context. It is important to pay attention to the things that the tests do not cover and that you may need to know about.

Here are a few examples of the more useful instruments and how relevant they may be to you in career development:

Type of Test	What it measures or shows	How it would apply in career development
RIASEC (Holland Code)	The six major families of skills	Identifying transferable skill set and roles
Strong Interest Inventory	Subjects or themes you are interested in	Career roles
Myers Briggs Type Indicator	Your preferences in relating to the world around you, information gathering, decision making and lifestyle. There are 16 personality types.	Identifying roles that suit your preferences
Cattells 16PF	Your traits and associated behaviour	Can help in assessing work environments or roles
Gardner's Multiple Intelligences	Eight different types of intelligences	To give an idea of where your (Multiple) strengths lie

Tests on the Internet: A health warning!
There are thousands of tests and exercises available on the internet; they vary greatly in reliability. Do your research. A few useful websites are listed in the reference section at the back of this book.

Examining your role models

Imitation is a very important part of our development; we learn our first language, not from textbooks, but by imitating the speech of those around us. It is said that organisations are places where people copy behaviour from each other — and that bad work habits are more successfully copied than good.

Activity 6
Analyse your role models

Consider the two or three people in your life who have influenced you most

→ What did they know most about?
→ What skills did they have to a very high level?
→ How would you describe them to someone else?
→ What did they teach you?
→ How are you like them? Even in small ways

Name	What they knew, what they could do well	What they taught me	How I am like them

e.g. John Smith taught me a lot about Computing and to look for the hidden opportunity. I am like him in that I have a good memory for detail.

Why do I need this?
To identify supporters, patrons and allies in your life from whom you have already learned so much.

Chapter 2 Summary

Add these to your list of problems for your career detection process:

1 Successful career management involves balancing sustainability (marketability) and vision

2 Career and life balance involves the components of working, learning, playing and giving (in relationships)

3 Stress is a given in the 21st century workplace. The best coping strategies are physical, emotional, playful and reflective ones

4 Separate the things you can change from the things you can't. Action those you can

5 Use ability and personality tests judiciously to put your abilities, preferences, traits and behaviours in context to help you identify your ideal roles

Activity 7
List some specific actions to make this happen:

	Action	Date	Desired outcome
1			
2			
3			

Activity 8
Revisit the WHY box on your career blue print to ensure that your success statement includes element of effective work and life balance. Make any necessary changes.

3

WHAT can I do?
(Identifying your
SKILLS and ROLE)

Chapter 3 outline
Identifying your transferable skills

→ What are skills?
→ Why are skills so important?
→ What do I use my skills on?
→ What are traits?
→ Three ways to find your skills set
→ The six families of skills
→ Skills levels
→ Producing your top skills list
→ Identifying your ROLE from your skills

Introduction

To identify your most suitable role you
will need to identify your transferable
skills set. A skill might be defined as
an action (or set of actions) that achieve
results. Transferable skills are core
skills that we use most of the time
to achieve our best results.

Most people do not know what their skills set is. Typically most people can name no more that 10 skills if you ask them what they do. However, using the exercises below you can expand the list to dozens or more!

Identifying your transferable skills

If you ask most people what their best skills are they usually can't tell you. If you press them they mention things like: "I am persistent, patient, goal-centred." These are useful things to be — but they are not skills. You need to understand also what you are doing when you are being so persistent!

What are Skills?

A **skill** is an action that will produce results with people, information or things. Skills may be very broadly defined as in **"Communication Skills"**, which covers a multitude of sub skills or as precisely defined as you can make it. The better your understanding of your skills sets the better will be your chance of identifying the best role for yourself.

Why are skills so important?

→ Skills are more marketable than traits; skills point to your achievements
→ Skills are the building blocks of your CV
→ HR managers look for achievements and skills when making decisions
→ Interviewers use competency frameworks — where they probe for skills
→ Knowing and doing is **not** the same thing! *So concentrate on doing!*

What do I use my skills on?

You need to identify your skills in terms of the things to which you apply them.

For example, **writing** is a skill — which usually has a specific object.

Writing letters =
skill (writing) + **object** (letters).

This may appear to be very basic but most CVs and job applications define skills sets too loosely to be of any use to the potential employer — who is interested more in the results you can achieve using those skills. Identifying a skill, no matter how precisely it is done, is only one third of the work. If you list presenting as a skill, this ignores the range of subjects where your skills may be applied. Therefore there is a need to identify the precise object (or range of objects) for the particular skill.

For example:
If your favourite is **Presenting**.

You need to know **what** *do you present and how* you *present it?*

There are degrees of precision in defining a core skill

→ **Imprecisely defined object** = presenting *anything*

→ **More precisely defined** = presenting *complex financial data*

→ **Most precisely defined** = presenting complex financial data *succinctly*

What are Traits?

If you are identifying your skills you need to be clear about the difference between skills and traits (or attributes). A trait or an attribute is a word describing the way in which we use a particular skill: E.g. Adjectives: Enthusiastic, precise, Adverbs: Carefully, patiently, Traits can point us to skills if we ask the question — what were we doing when we were being that enthusiastic or careful? The answer will come back as a word usually ending in —'ing' - such a word is a skills word.

The most marketable traits:

→ Honesty   → Reliability

→ Consistency   → Enthusiasm

Activity 1
My Favourite Traits

List your favourite traits:
Prioritise the ones that would be most useful to *you* in your career.

Here's a list to get you started:

→ Pleasant   → Charming

→ Honest   → Ingenious

→ Clever   → Witty

→ Persistent   → Thorough

→ Creative   → Consistent

→ Rigorous   → Diligent

→ Inclusive   → Warm

→ Reserved   → Numerate

→ Aware   → Comprehensive

→ Organised   → Wise

My Favourite Traits (how my work is described)

1	2	3	4	5

 When you are done, enter your favourite traits in the WHAT box on the Career Blueprint (at the end of the book).

Why do I need this?
To help you understand how others see you. A good reality check to see if the perception matches the reality.

Three ways to find your skills set.

Activity 2
Finding your skills set from your traits

(Traits are the clues that lead you to your skills!)

List a number of your traits and convert them to skills - I have given you one sample:

You can convert your favourite traits to skills by asking the question?

What were you actually doing when you were acting reliably?

Trait	Skill(s) used when demonstrating this trait
Reliable	Accounting, paying, notifying etc.

Why do I need this?
It is important to be able to distinguish between traits and skills at all stages of the process. Traits are general descriptions and show how we operate. Skills are more precise and show what we can do.

Activity 3
Finding your skills set from your life story

(More detective work! What's your record? What have you done?)

Identify incidents in your life when you achieved results you were proud of. Write each one of these as one page listing out the following:

→ **Your objective**
   What you were trying to achieve

→ **Your obstacles**
   What stood in your way

→ **Your actions**
   What you did — focussing on the skills you used make sure the words end in *"ing"* — this gives you the skills words — rule a separate column for these

→ **Your outcome**
   What you actually achieved.

Read your story over to a friend - get them to write down the skills words.

This is a very useful exercise because it uses the same structure interviewers use in competency interviews (see page 52).

This example should help:

Your objective	To build a garden shed from a DIY Kit	
Your obstacles	I am not into DIY, we were running out of space in the house and my partner was threatening divorce!	
Your actions	I read the plans. I checked all the items in the box. I assembled all the tools I needed. I dug the foundations .. etc	**Skills words** Reading Checking Assembling Digging Etc.
Your outcome	I got the shed up in an afternoon and saved about €300 and saved my marriage	

TIP: *Ask a friend to listen to your story and quiz you on what you did — with the objective of extracting as many skills as possible. You will be surprised at the results.*

Why do I need this?
Transferable skills are the building blocks of your career. If you know your skills you can more easily identify what makes you effective and how you get results.

Now fill this in for your story:

Your objective		
Your obstacles		
Your actions		**Skills words**
Your outcome		

Activity 4
Finding your skills set from previous jobs:

You can do this in at least four ways:

1 Analyse a work project in the same way as you did for a life experience in (2) above

2 Go through your job descriptions — they will be peppered with skills words

3 Recall any performance reviews or things you were praised for — these judgments will include skills words somewhere.

4 Recall things you were regularly called upon to do. These will not only identify the skills words but will show you the more marketable ones!

Skills words in job descriptions	
Skills words from performance reviews	
Skills words in my tasks (on request)	

Why do I need this?
Past achievement is a reliable indicator of future performance.

Handy hint:
Remember skills words end with the letters "ing"!
A skill is an "ING" thing!

The six families of skills

As you do more work discovering your skills sets you will find it handy to divide skills into logical families.

❶ PHYSICAL SKILLS:
→ The first major family of skills is that dealing with technology, equipment, plants, animals or skills involving our senses.
Typical skills words in this category: Making (furniture), repairing (kettles), installing

❷ INFORMATION SKILLS
→ The second family of skills deals with collecting and analysing data of all sorts.
Typical skills words in this category: Researching, Analysing, Deciding

❸ INTERPERSONAL SKILLS
→ This deals with all our interpersonal skills which we use in one-to-one situations or in groups.
Typical skills words in this category: Helping, Listening, Persuading, Collaborating

❹ CREATIVE SKILLS
→ These are skills we use to create or adapt things.
Typical skills words in this category: Designing, Adapting, Transforming, Drawing, Painting

❺ MANAGERIAL SKILLS
→ These are the skills we use when we lead people or get things done.
Typical skills words: Supervising, Motivating, Selling, Changing

❻ ADMINISTRATIVE SKILLS
→ The last category of skills involves what we do to keep things running smoothly.
Typical skills words: Listing, Co-ordinating, Counting, Classifying, Checking

Why our skills are not apparent to us

Most people are only barely aware of the range and depth of their own skill set.

A helpful way to raise awareness is to examine the four stage of learning as below:

These are:
❶ "I don't know that I don't know" - This is when you think anybody can do anything!

It is technically called UNCONSCIOUS INCOMPETENCE

❷ "I know that I don't know" - When you find out that it's not as easy as it looks

– Called CONSCIOUS INCOMPETENCE

③ "I know that I know" – when you learn your skills and build up your level

– Called CONSCIOUS COMPETENCE

④ "I don't know that I know" – When you are so competent you can perform well without thinking it! - This stage is then called UNCONSCIOUS COMPETENCE

The diagram below explains what happens.

So the result of this strange phenomenon is firstly that we don't know that we know, we don't know how we learned, and worst of all, we don't know how to repeat the experience because we have no memory of it! Unless, of course, we take the time to find out. How do we get around this problem? How do we access the memories of skills? If two of the phases involve consciousness, can we recover these? It is said that the brain retains everything that it records – the only difficulty is in the rate and method of recovery which seems to get less and less reliable as we grow older. We get around this problem by story telling. The stories we tell are about things we have done and a good story starts off with a challenge, a list of the obstacles to be faced, what we did and the results achieved. If we tell that story to ourselves we will get one result. If we tell the story to others and ask them to listen out for the skills contained in our story the results will be much more comprehensive.

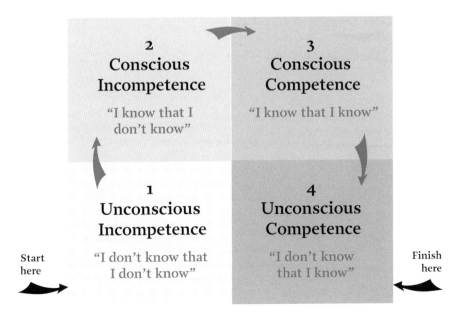

2
Conscious Incompetence

"I know that I don't know"

3
Conscious Competence

"I know that I know"

1
Unconscious Incompetence

Start here

"I don't know that I don't know"

4
Unconscious Competence

"I don't know that I know"

Finish here

A recent trend in job interviewing: Competency interviews

In the last few years many interviewers have gone over to a form of interviewing which asks for examples where interviewees have used their skills. The structure they use has three Phases:

1. PROBLEM   2. ACTIONS   3. RESULTS.

Does this look familiar?
To prepare for such interviews candidates need to identify the depth and breadth of their experiences with the skills sets of the job for which they are applying.

If you are stuck in identifying your skills set try this:

1 Look at the type of equipment or technology you like to use — this will help you identify your **physical** skills

2 Look at your library, books, magazines, favourite websites — this may give you clues about your **informational skills**

3 Think of ways in which you like to be creative — this will access your **creative** skills

4 Think about the way others relate to you, or ask for your help — this will give you clues about your **interpersonal skills**

5 Identify situations where you took the lead (or were asked to) — particularly if others were reluctant to get involved —

this will give you data about your **managerial skills**

6 Itemise the situations where you have had to write things down, calculate or classify things — this will identify your **administrative skills**

Skills levels

As you inventory your skills you will notice that certain skills, such as recording are not as complex or as difficult to acquire as higher level skills such as analysing data.

You will need to:

a Maximise the list of skills that you have and
b Sort those skills into those that are highest level
c Identify those that you are enthusiastic about using
d Research which ones are the most marketable

Some higher level skills with people, like leading or mentoring or guiding comprise dozens or more other skills or sub-skills. It is very easy to get lost in a forest of skills so naming, classification and prioritisation needs to be done.

You would also need to think about the level at which your skills operate

→ Learner
→ Average level
→ Professional

If you are at learner or average skills level you may need to re-consider training and development as part of your career plan going forward.

Producing your top skills list

When you have researched your best examples prioritise your skills according to level and liking.

What are my top skills?

Ones which meet all or most of these criteria:

I love using these skills, I like learning about them, they come easily to me and they would be useful in the world of work.

Here are some examples (Not all for the same person!)

	1	2	3	4	5
Skill	Restoring	Writing	Motivating	Playing	Counselling
Object	Furniture	Proposals	Sales Staff	Keyboards	Students
Trait	Sensitively	Concisely	Effectively	Precisely	Empathetically

For each of your favourite skills you will need to clarify it further under the following headings:

1 Skill name	2 Preferred object	3 Trait	4 Skills type	5 Level	6 Marketability 1=Very good 2=OK 3=Needs Training
Restoring	Furniture	Sensitively	Physical	Master Craftsperson 10 years experience	Level 1 In heavy demand!

Why do I need this?
Good CVs are built up from clearly identified skills sets. At interviews you will be better able to identify what you can achieve in your chosen role.

Activity 5 — *Fill one in for yourself!*

Master Skills Template. Here is a template for you to fill out.

	1	2	3	4	5
Skill Name					
Preferred Object: *I like using this skill with*					
Skills type *1					
Skill Level *How proficient are you at it?*2					
Marketability *(e.g. "in demand") etc.*					

*1: PHYSICAL INFORMATIONAL INTERPERSONAL CREATIVE MANAGERIAL ADMINISTRATIVE

*2: 1=Very good
2=Ok
3=Needs Training

 Enter the information about your skills and objects into the WHAT box of your Career Blueprint

Activity 6
Identifying your ROLE from your skills

Your role can be deduced from your list of four or five top skills e g. someone who is good at leading, setting goals, supporting and motivating people could be called a MANAGER or a TEAM LEADER.

How to find potential roles (or jobs) from skills.

If you can identify your core skills set precisely to include the most marketable skills you enjoy using then you can use this information to guide your research and your assessment of potential offers.

In your researches ask yourself and others the question:

→ **What do you call somebody with this skills set?**

In assessing potential job offers ask the question:

→ **How well does this job description match my top skills set?**

Activity 7

Do some creative thinking about HOW your top skills could be combined in different ways to suggest different roles and enter your favourites on your Blueprint.

e.g. combining the following skills:

Motivating+supporting+setting (goals)+ innovating

Could give you the following alternative roles (and careers):

Film Director, Marketing Executive, Politician, Project Design Manager etc.

Your top 5 skills and some possible roles:

Your top 5 skills	Possible roles
1	
2	
3	
4	

Why do I need this?
To show that you have options not immediately apparent to you.

Hint:
Use an internet search engine to find jobs that match your five top skills — enter them in the search line and the system should return sites or pages that contain those skills. *Be patient!*

In the next chapter roles will be discovered through your interests.

Chapter 3 Summary

As a career detective you now know the following:

❶ Skills need to be precisely defined in terms of the action, the object (what you use the skill on) and the attribute (how you use the skill)

❷ Traits are useful in describing how you operate but employers are more interested in the how you use your skills to achieve results

❸ Our best skills are hidden from us in the way our mind works — our brain "forgets" how it learned

❹ Explore your life and career to date to find examples of the skills you used

❺ We need to do a reality check on our perceived skills set to ensure they are at the right level — if we are offering them to the market

Activity 8

List some specific goals you can set about enabling your career to move forward:

	Action	Date	Desired outcome
1			
2			
3			

WHAT do I know? (Identifying your FIELD)

4

Chapter 4 outline
Finding your expertise
and where it can be used

→   What do you know? What interests you?

→   How you learn — the value of experience

→   Benchmarking your level of expertise

→   The choices: *to specialise* or
     to be a generalist?

→   Brainstorming your level of expertise

→   Combining expertise and skills

Introduction

It is said that we live in a knowledge-driven economy. It is not just a matter of what you can do — but also what you know and how you combine the two in a career that suits and energises you.

What do you know? What interests you?

What are you really interested in? Would you like to make it your career?

You might not consider yourself an expert at first — but if you are interested in a subject and motivated to find out about it then, in time, you can become an expert because your degree of enthusiasm and engagement with the subject will mark you out and opens doors for you.

> *Hint:*
> In this chapter world "field" will be used to refer both to field of knowledge (expertise) and field of activity (industry or sector) — the context will make the meaning clear.

Once you are clear where you want to grow your expertise you are then looking for is a **FIELD of ACTIVITY** that will use it.

If CAREER= ROLE + FIELD then your field of activity is primarily determined by your expertise. (We saw in the last chapter that understanding your skills set can help to identify your ROLE). Understanding what you have both in terms of knowledge and skill can deepen your understanding of what makes you effective and opens up more career options.

How you learn: The value of experience

It would be worth reviewing what you have learned through experience — including skills or subjects you taught yourself. If your experience with the school or college system was difficult or mixed it is likely that you learned in different ways to those of your teachers.

Multiple routes to learning.

Adults learn in the following ways: *If they want to, if they need to, if it is relevant to them or if it checks out with their prior experience.*

There are various schools of thought in classifying types of learning. One method is to classify learners as follows:

→ **Activists:**
  Those who are constantly looking for something new to stimulate them

→ **Theorists:**
  Those who need to see the unifying theories behind things

→ **Reflectors:**
  Those who soak up data like sponges

→ **Pragmatists:**
  Those who learn things only if it is practical and relevant to their situation

Most people learn using a combination of the above. How do you learn the important things in your life? For example, how did you master the last gadget you bought? Did you read the manual and carefully follow the instructions – or did you experiment with it using a combination of intuition and logic until you got it to work.

CASE STUDY from the MUSIC BUSINESS:

Most rock guitarists learned their instruments by imitating records and playing with others; few learned their instruments from text books!

Activity 1
How did you do your learning?

List the subject that you are enthusiastic about and list how you learned them. Which of these were self-taught?

Subject	How you learned it?
1	
2	
3	
4	

Why do I need this?
Not all learning takes place at school! We all have powerful self-teaching skills. (How did you learn things growing up?

Finding your expertise and where it can be used

It is useful to take a broad view of the subjects you know about.

Activity

Draw up your own interest inventory based on the following:

→ Subjects you studied and are have qualifications for

→ Subjects you have acquired a working knowledge of in your job

→ Processes and procedures you have in-depth knowledge of because of your work

Consider also other forms of knowledge:

→ Types of problems that you can solve

→ Your contacts – who you know, what they can do

→ Societies or networks you belong to

Activity 2

(Suggestion:
Use a large sheet of paper – you could be surprised how much you know!)

Subject that interest you	Problems you can solve	Networks/contacts available to you

Why do I need this?
To show the knowledge that you have and the knowledge that you have access through your contacts

Benchmarking your level of expertise

Consider the level of your knowledge in those subjects that interest you – how would you rate your level of knowledge? Casual amateur –professional?

→ *What's unique about your knowledge?*
There may be a particular value in the fact that you are the only person in the world with an interest in a particular subject. Is this knowledge commercially valuable? Ask yourself the question – what is the reason that this subject is so little sought-after? A dead-end, perhaps, or of no commercial value?

→ *What is the current state of play in the field you are interested in? –*
Is it well-established or in the process of development or in transition? If it is well-established then entry to the field may be very strictly regulated. If it is expanding or in a state of flux there may be opportunities

→ *How difficult or challenging is this field, for you or others?*
Some fields, such as medicine, are attractive to many but are notoriously difficult to get into and qualify. It is worth researching the dropout or burnout rate

→ *Have you a particular talent or taste for the field that others don't have?*
It is worth reviewing your own connection with your favourite field – when you discovered it did you take to it like a duck to water? How did it engage you compared to others - for you, is it a field of particular fascination?

→ *How would you be considered by others in the field?*
Be realistic as to how others who are expert in the field would assess your level of knowledge. Look for honest feedback from all available sources

→ *What level of certification is needed?*
Increasingly, many fields require various forms of entry certification. However, it may be worth researching the options around certification – some routes are better and cheaper than others - even in the same profession

→ *Just how motivated are you?*
Evidence of your motivation would be those subjects that you taught yourself – or which you have researched independently

→ *Is there further development needed?*
Once you have considered all of the above you may decide

that further education is needed — however you attain it. You have the choice of attending courses, learning via the internet, becoming involved in a hands-on way through experience. Choose the route to learning that best suits you

The choices:
To specialise or *to be a generalist?*

It is obvious that to have specialist knowledge in an area that is commercially "hot" is a good insurance for the future. Career paths are initially more obvious for specialists and it is true that the education system is better designed to turn out specialists. However, the more specialised you become the fewer people will understand you. The danger in a complex work environment the specialists may not be able to communicate with each other. Organisations are rarely run by specialists but by people who can manage them!

As a generalist you may find that your knowledge is too broad and superficial to be of use in your chosen field so you then have to choose to specialise.

You might like to consider the following questions:

❶ Do I see myself as a specialist? Or are my interests broad?

❷ Do I see myself remaining in this specialism for ever?

❸ Is the specialism one that is static, or ever-changing?

❹ What's the future of this specialism in the market place?

How do you see your role changing in the long term?

CASE STUDY:
The Media Business

There is a vast plethora of graduates on the market who hold degrees in media studies — and who acquired them in the vain hope that their degree would open the door to rewarding occupations. While qualifications are useful the reality of the media business (especially broadcasting) is that high levels of reward and pay only occur when a brilliant idea is made into a commercially viable product. The really highly-sought after expertise is the one of creating commercially viable ideas and bringing them to fruition. Most graduates are not taught this and many lack that vital spark.

Activity 3

Rate your four top subjects, which you are enthusiastic about — and benchmark them.

Subject	Your level of accomplishment	How did you learn best?	What further development do I need?
1			
2			
3			
4			

***Why do I need this?* Reality check! It is critical to differentiate between casual and professional interests.**

You have now identified your top subjects, how you learned them and the level at which you operate you now have a basis on which to explore realistic career options.

 Enter your four favourite subjects on the Career Blueprint in the WHERE box

Brainstorming your expertise to identify your favourite fields

Now that you are clear on your interests and you have benchmarked your expertise

you can move on to identify the fields of activity that could use these. The challenge is to be very specific in what you are interested in. The mistake many people make is being open to everything and wanting to try everything. The result of this is that you will drift from one entry-level job to another.

The one-subject approach

Imagine you were the world expert on nutrition — what fields of activity would be interested in talking to you — to seek your involvement and offer you a career? Here are some possibilities:

Brainstorm the possible alternative **fields:**
→ International Aid agencies
→ Agriculture
→ Public Health
→ Food manufacturing

If you had your choice of organisations you could also have your choice of **roles.**

You could be, for example:
→ An expert
→ A lecturer
→ Chief executive
→ Head of Research

Hint:
You could brainstorm the possible combinations for the four fields above with the four roles — sixteen in all. You could, for example, be an expert in the field of International Aid Agencies or be Chief Executive in the field of Public Health etc.
Which appeal to you?
Which exist in reality?)

Everybody is into computers nowadays, but where are the jobs?

Take a very general discipline (like computing) and ask yourself — what types of organisation would use this knowledge? The answer is every type of organisation because everybody uses computers in business. Now identify your area of interest and expertise e.g. structured database programming and you narrow the area of search considerably.

Activity 4

If I were the world expert in MY favourite subject what fields of activity would be open to me?

Subject	Fields of ACTIVITY open to me
	1
	2
	3 etc.

Why do I need this?
**To show that you have
options not immediately
apparent to you.**

Now that you have identified
the fields of activity you are
faced with the that there could
be hundreds of possible roles
you could occupy. To cut the
field down further you could
consider defining your area of
expertise much more precisely.
E.g." I am the world's expert
on the major faults in the XXX
Programme for controlling
industrial sampling
in petro-chemicals."

Combining your favourite subjects to generate options.

Most jobs combine several
strands of expertise. Examine
how your favourite subjects
could work in combination. Take
two subjects e.g. economics and
marketing and identify the types
of organisation which uses and
values this expertise. Explore
the options.

If you add another subject
(e.g. languages) and you will find
the area narrows considerably.

Combining three subjects

Most jobs now require a working
knowledge of computers. Add
to this any other subject you are
interested/expert in:
Example: Internet + German
Language = On-line translation
services, web-support into
German-speaking market

If you have an interest in marketing
as well you could combine the three
subjects as follows:

Internet + German + Marketing
= On-line translation services
or On-line selling to the
German-speaking market.

Hint:
**Use Venn diagrams to work
out the possibilities**

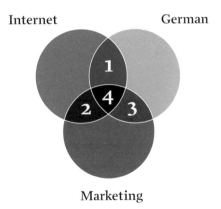

You will now have four new areas
of opportunity to work on:

Fields combining	Types of organisation
1 Internet + German	All German businesses etc.
2 German + Marketing	German businesses interested in expanding their business
3 Marketing + Internet	Internet search companies
4 German + Marketing + Internet	German-speaking businesses interested in expanding their markets on the net etc.

Activity 5
Combine three areas you are interested in as above

Fields combining	Types of organisations	Reality check (how many, how accessible?)
1		
2		
3		
4		

Why do I need this?
To expand the areas of possibility open to you.

Getting experience: Internships etc.

If the field is interested in your expertise but not willing to pay it would be worth considering the following options:

→ Developing a higher level of expertise

→ Joining an intern programme

→ Doing pro-bono work in this area – but using some other job or role to pay the bills

→ Involving yourself in this area as a hobby

→ Researching the reasons why expertise is not paid for according to your specifications

Combining expertise and skills

To reduce the numbers of possibilities you could focus on roles that might be offered to you.

If you have identified your top transferable skills (see Chapter 3) you can match those skills to possible roles (jobs) in the organisations that value your expertise. If you are researching opportunities the question then is: *"I am interested in the field of X- My top skills are A, B and C. In your experience what do you call someone in this field that has these skills on their job specification?* So at the end of this chapter you should have an idea of your favourite subjects and the fields of activity that would reward them.

Activity 6
Possible fields of activity and some possible roles.

Possible Fields of Activity	Possible Roles
1	
2	
3	
4	
5	

Why do I need this?
To show that you have options not immediately apparent to you and to narrow the field.

 Reflect on possible FIELDS of activity and the ROLES that would suit your expertise and enter your favourites on the Career Blueprint in the WHERE? Boxes.

Chapter 4 Summary

For the career detective knowledge is power. What you know, who you know and where it's all happening are all part of your future.

Consider the following tasks:

1 Do an inventory of your areas of interest. List other areas of knowledge apart from the purely academic: Practical hands-on experience, procedural knowledge, contacts etc

2 Consider whether you are a specialist or a generalist. You could also be a specialist who will combine your specialism with another subject, in time, to create a new field of activity

3 Benchmark them in terms of level: Amateur, student, expert, professional

4 Understand your own process of learning; you might be interested in theories or what works in practice, or what is relevant to you or you might even have a particular fascination for a specific subject that nobody else shares

5 Rely on what you have learned through experience

6 The more precisely you define what you know about the easier it will be to define fields of activity which could use that knowledge

Activity 7:
List some specific actions to make this happen.

	Action	Date	Desired outcome
1			
2			
3			

WHERE can I go?

5

Chapter 5 outline
What are the working conditions that best suit you?

→ Hell at work - what stops you performing
→ Heaven at work - what gets you going
→ Resources for finding organisations
→ Approaching organisations
→ Promoting yourself:
   Creative alternatives to the CV

Introduction

To do your best work your working
conditions need to be optimum —
good support from colleagues,
recognition for your effort and progress
upwards at the right time for you.
More career changes occur because
of working conditions than because
of money. In the previous chapter we
identified your fields of activity through
your interests. In this chapter we
develop the process of finding the type
of organisation or environment that
will suit you by looking at some of the
factors that can make the difference in
helping you perform on the job.

What are the working conditions that best suit you?

One of the most frequently-quoted statistics about people at work is that one in two people are in the wrong job! Most people choose to do nothing about this tragic situation. Imagine trying to compete in a sport for which you were not suited and being expected to win a gold medal at the Olympics; this is what happens when we sign up to a job that doesn't suit us.

> **According to a recent study only one in three workers consider that their work is adequately recognized — most consider that it rarely is.**
>
> **Another survey found that over one in six employees had seriously considered sabotaging their workplace in the previous year.**

Experts in motivation draw a distinction between two elements of motivation at work:

→ **Hygiene Factors:**
These are the things that lead to dissatisfaction e.g. working conditions, equipment etc. People will strive to achieve 'hygiene' needs because they are unhappy without them. However, if they meet these needs the satisfaction is short-lived

→ **Motivators:** These are the items that are found to motivate people in the long-term: Personal growth, Opportunities for professional and personal development, Advancement, Recognition... which represent a far deeper level of meaning and fulfilment

If the basics are not right the job can become a living hell.

Hell at work - What stops you performing?

Here are some of the major blocks to performance in the 21st century:

→ Unclear goal setting by management

→ Unrealistic expectations

→ Micro-management

→ Lack of recognition and opportunities for advancement

→ Lack of proper resources

→ Long working hours

→ Bullying, harassment and discrimination in the workplace

→ Lack of long-term job security

You may have your own favourites...

Heaven at work — What gets you going?

Numerous studies show that people expect the following at work:

→ Fairness in reward system

→ Trust and integrity

→ Respect

→ Recognition for special effort

→ Support

→ On-going meaningful feedback

→ To be consulted about matters relating to their own work

→ Opportunities for variety, creativity and discretion in their work

→ Opportunities for advancement

Which are the most relevant for you?

Reflect on successful work experience where you did something that got you noticed or promoted:

How did the working conditions help you?
How did your boss or colleagues support, recognise or help you?

FACT
More people switch jobs or career because of people factors at work —either because of the way the were managed (or not!) or because of organisational politics or culture ("that's the way things are done around here!").

Activity 1
Finding Heaven at work

❶ Identify in the left hand column things that make life hell for you at work. For example you may have to deal with bad premises, slow technology, bureaucracy etc

❷ For each irritant there may be a number of different opposites for example your hell at work may be office politics. One opposite of this may an organisation that has no politics — but such an organisation probably does not exist. Think about what you really are looking for when you reject office politics — are you really looking for fairness, inclusion or consultation

❸ Pick the option that suits you best and write it into the right hand column

❹ Identify the four or five items that would be essential in your ideal work environment

	These things turn work into HELL		These things make work HEAVEN
1			
2			
3			
4			
5			
6			
7			
8			
9			
10			

Identify the best conditions for you. Put an asterisk (*) in this column beside the items that are non-negotiable — if you were changing your job.

Select the top four and enter them in the WHERE box on the Career Blueprint.

Why do I need this?
To ensure that the conditions are right for you at work so that you can perform to the level of your best ability.

Resources for finding organisations

Apart from the obvious one of trawling the internet consider the following:

❶ The yellow pages (golden pages) in your local phone directory. The entries are arranged by subject and give an indication of active business during the last 12 month period. Ads can also give you clues as to the size, products and services of your target organisations

❷ Use your network by asking focussed questions with the objective of identifying those organisations which may value your expertise or skills.

❸ Consider attending presentations by trade organisations and, over time, generating a profile and an interest in a specific sector

Approaching organisations

Least effective ways

❶ Sending unsolicited CVs (résumés). Most (over 90%) are never read.

❷ Answering job ads. They have poor rate of return

❸ Job searching on the internet – many sites are out of date and not maintained properly. Internet job searching is at its best in the Information Technology interest.

❹ Being too general in your approach ("have you any jobs? I'll consider anything.")

❺ Being aggressive in your approaches

Most effective ways

❶ Establishing what an organisation is looking for, how it recruits staff and timing your approach properly

❷ Using your contacts selectively and effectively by asking focussed targeted questions

Promoting yourself: *Creative alternatives to the CV*

❶ Identify a specific job/role in an organisation that interests you. Write to the manager/ executive in charge of that area pointing your skills and expertise and how they match the demands of that role

❷ Target specific organisations. Research what is happening in their business – write a short paper making suggestions for problems they may be encountering in a field where you have proven expertise and can offer solutions

3 Networking in depth to find out what is happening in a field of your choice – become familiar with the jargon and current challenges in your chosen fields of interest

Chapter 5 Summary

1 As career detective you are now on the trail. However, to make sure you get into the right places you need to ensure the following are done

2 In finding the right career for yourself distinguish between things which will lead to lasting motivation rather than those which will just eliminate dissatisfaction

3 Identify what you don't want, then identify the best options for you– just don't settle for the "obvious opposites"

4 Identify what is non-negotiable for you in finding the ideal career for you.

5 Ask yourself what industries or fields use combinations of your areas of interest

6 Target organisations very specifically

Activity 2
List some specific actions to make this happen.

	Action	Date	Desired outcome
1			
2			
3			

HOW committed are you?

6

Chapter 6 outline
Success in career management =

→ Attitude + Behaviour + Commitment
→ Getting your attitude on track
→ What is your behaviour?
→ How committed are you?
→ Managing your weaknesses
→ Using your two brains in tandem:
The Logical (left) brain and the Creative
(right) brain

Introduction

Success in your career means managing the one thing you have exclusive control over and responsibility for: Your attitude. You must want to succeed and to be prepared for the hard work that it will take. Your unique success depends on your will to succeed, your focus and your commitment to the things that are really important.

"Current cultural values gives people the idea that they should receive everything without a personal effort... if something goes wrong, the cause has to be looked for in some external agency"
Prof Paul Verhaeghe,
University of Ghent, 2007.

How your attitude drives the process along: *The Choice is Yours...*

Your attitude is the key in moving your career plan forward. The choice is yours - you can wait for the breaks or create some of them by putting your best energy with confidence into working on yourself. You have all the resources you need.

Thinking Point
Some people reserve their best efforts for planning their holidays, parties or weddings and then put their organising and other skills on hold thereafter. Where do you apply your best efforts?

There are many people who would be cynical about their prospects the pessimists; this process is not for them because they see the glass as being half-empty, and things are always getting worse! The optimists see that there is something in the glass but they have yet to realise its full potential. Optimists usually achieve more, learn more and have more fun. Your approach, commitment and belief in your own capabilities is what will determine the difference between success and failure. You may need to check out just how committed you are and how badly you want real change.

Case Study: Toxic Ted

Ted spent four years doing a degree course in marketing without researching the area properly. He has made some half-hearted attempts to apply for jobs but fails because his lack of energy and focus does not impress potential employers or contacts. He is not aware of the impact his negative energy has on people around him. For him it is all someone else's fault. Any Toxic Teds in your life?

Success in career management = Attitude + Behaviour + Commitment

Identifying your Career ABC

A: ATTITUDE What's your attitude? To career? To life?

"When the winds of change blow some people build walls, others build windmills "

(Dr. Peter Hawkins)

Check your attitude: *Which list applies to you?*

List 1	List 2
I am a victim of circumstance	I am the architect of my future
I need support	I am a resource for others
Powerless	Powerful
A voice in the wilderness	A voice that is heard
I tend to look for reasons not to do things	I tend to look for opportunities
I believe some people are born lucky	I believe those who work hardest have better luck
Ultimately we are all on our own	We need each other to survive
Nobody knows the trouble I've seen	Other peoples' struggles are just as tough as mine
Things are getting worse	The world is as bad/good as it ever was
Why bother?	Why not?

Which list do you wish to live by?

Activity 1:

Write the names/initials of people in your life who fit into either list:

	List 1	Are they successful?	List 2	Are they successful?
1				
2				
3				

Why do I need this? Our role models inspire us.

Which of these would be better role models for you?

Getting your attitude on track.

Activity 2
If only... Identify five things in your life you wish had been different:

If only...... (I hadn't been born left-handed etc.)

1	
2	
3	
4	
5	

If you repeated this exercise every day for a month how do you think you would feel?

To get back on track Identify things in your life that you are truly thankful for **today.**

I am thankful that... (*I am in good health etc.*)

1	
2	
3	
4	
5	

If you repeated *this* exercise every day for a month, how do you think you would feel?

B: BEHAVIOUR
What is your behaviour?

Do you wait for things to happen or make them happen?

"It is easier to act ourselves into a new way of thinking than to think ourselves into a new way of doing."
Goethe *(author of Faust) – 19th century*

"Don't talk about it. Just do it!" – 21st century career coach.

Proactive?   Reactive?

Be prepared to be an activist in your career development. A critical attribute of effective managers is proactivity. Get used to acting proactively! Every day do something to move your career plans forward. Multiple small steps on a regular basis build up the proactive habit and are more enduring that occasional "heaves!"

Activity 3
List three actions you will take to move your career plan today.

1	
2	
3	

To make them happen-Record them, tell somebody about them and celebrate them when they have happened.

Why do I need this? **To give you practice in becoming pro-active.**

C: COMMITMENT
How committed are you?

Nobody would run a marathon or compete at a serious level in sport without a structured regime of training but many are unwilling to apply similar effort to maintaining or changing their career. If you are not prepared to commit to a similar level of effort your career will not progress as it should. For the process to succeed you **must** set goals – every goal-setting book says that. *If you fail to plan,* *you are planning to fail.* However, the goals need to be judiciously set. If you over-estimate you will fail, if you under-estimate your goals you will continue as you are.

Traditionally managers define goals that are SMART

Specific Measurable Achievable Realistic Time-bound

However, if you set goals in this format you may lose the benefit of **Stretch Goals** which you **really** want to achieve, and you are committed to − but you are not quite sure just how you will achieve them. It might be worth thinking back to times in your life when you did not see

obstacles that pre-occupy you just now.

Another aspect of achieving the goal is **relevance**. Is this goal really relevant to you? There is no percentage in trying to achieve other peoples' goals. It is said, that a powerful force in the lives of children is the unlived lives of their parents.

Another technique is **negative motivation**. Consider the things you do not want to happen in your life. What would you have to do to make sure that they did not happen? Set your goals to ensure that the unwanted does not occur!

Focus on **needs** rather than **wants.**

Activity 4

List three things you do not want to happen in your career:

I do not want this to happen in my career	What I have to do to ensure this does not happen?
1	
2	
3	

Why do I need this?
Don't under-estimate the power of negative motivation.

We shall re-visit goal-setting in the final chapter.

Managing your weaknesses

We need to identify clearly the areas where our skills and expertise are properly developed. We also need to develop those things we do not find as easy to master as others and accept how to do deal with them – so that we do not have unrealistic expectations of ourselves.

Activity 5
How I have overcome weakness

Areas in which I have to struggle compared to other people	How I have managed this
1	
2	
3	

Why do I need this?
Why do I need this? To identify your coping mechanisms.

Avoid making these a central part of your plan unless you have no choice. Be aware that they will require high levels of maintenance!

Managing your weaknesses

Using your two brains in tandem: The Logical (left) brain and the Creative (right) brain.

Using your two brains in tandem:

The Logical (left) brain and the Creative (right) brain
Our brain is a complex organ with conscious and subconscious elements. The brain is generally divided into two hemispheres - LEFT and RIGHT – which operate in very different ways. The left brain controls the right side of the body and the right brain controls the left side.

Some functions are found on both sides of the brain but it is more useful to think of it as operating in two distinct ways - LEFT BRAIN mode and RIGHT BRAIN mode.

Left brain is best at	Right brain is best at
→ Assembling data into a logical sequence → Detail → Reality checking → Keeping you safe → Building up good habits of behaviour and thinking → Using the senses → Dealing with time → Words → Practical matters	→ Seeing patterns in data → Identifying possibilities → Can help make your vision a reality → Improving your energy and self-motivation → Dealing with ambiguity → Using sensuality → Experimentation → Seeing the fun in things → Dealing with space → Dealing with the subconscious

However, both brains have limitations which you need to be aware of;

Left brain limitations	Right brain limitations
→ Sometimes restricted by seeing limits and flaws. → Can be a slave of habit and tradition → Plays old scripts: "You're too old etc." → Punishes mistakes → Has to get it all right → Can rationalise anything it wants to!	→ Misses vital details → Can lose contact with reality → Can take things out of context → Not good at action planning → Often cannot settle down to business

You need both parts of the brain working in tandem to help you move forward. It is a mistake to think of one mode of the brain as being better than others. However, if you are having trouble putting your plans into action you may have left brain problems.

Dealing with Left and Right Brain problems:

→ **How do you know when the Left Brain is too active?**

❶ You find yourself thinking too quickly

❷ You are overwhelmed by words.

❸ You have rationalised yourself into a state of inaction

Remedies: Get out into the open air, use exercise, meditate, and dance!

→ **How do you know when the Right Brain is too active?**

❶ Being over-optimistic - *"Nothing is a problem"*

❷ You cannot focus on details.

❸ You cannot prioritise items or connect the dots

Remedies: Write things down, ask somebody else to critique your plans, make action plans.

Using the subconscious brain in career development:

We know that the brain can solve problems subconsciously (e.g. leaving unsolved problems for a while — solutions can present themselves when we next see the problem!)

The brain works best in subconscious mode when you leave it question to work with

Example: *What other jobs beside my own have a similar skills set?*

Chapter 6 Summary

The best detectives have attitude — what's yours? Does it help? Does it get in the way of good things happening to you?

Remember:

1 Your own attitude is critical to success or failure in this process

2 Success is a combination of attitude with appropriate behaviours (actions) backed up by real commitment

3 You need to check that your attitude is not creating a self-fulfilling prophecy of failure

4 Action plans and goal-setting need to be regular parts of the process

5 Our left brain can help us by assessing our options but our right brain creates the vision to bring us forward

Now prove it:

Activity 6
List some specific actions to make things happen.

	Action	Date	Desired outcome
1			
2			
3			

Other thoughts:

7

WHO can help?

Chapter 7 outline
Working with others

→ Networking and 'Buddying'
→ Identifying your supports
→ The five types of contacts
→ The three types of interviews
→ Making an impression

Introduction

Career change is practically impossible without involving other people – you need help, support and information. The temptation is find people whose only role is to help and support you. The process will be much more effective if you can set up networks of people who help each other. Think of the success of BEBO and FACEBOOK on the net!

Working with others

Networking and 'Buddying': Why no-one is an island

One of the most difficult things to do is to see ourselves properly in proportion – most people sell themselves short and under-estimate their capacities, while others over-estimate themselves. You need feedback and information exchange to narrow the gap in perception between what you think about yourself and what others experience.

Networking and buddying is a two-way street. The best way to get contacts is to make it your strategy to support and encourage others. The most well-worn phrase in the business, and possibly the truest, is "what goes round comes round."

Identifying your supports

Identify what is on your shopping list for support: Select from the following list:

❶ Emotional support: To counter deficient self-confidence and reinforce positive messages

❷ Someone who can talk very openly about the deeper issues

❸ Information sources

❹ A sounding board to test your ideas

❺ Reality checking

❻ Someone with whom you can practice presentations

❼ Somebody to link you to others

❽ An advocate: Somebody to present your case for you to others

❾ Somebody with whom you can exchange support

Be selective in your choice of support. It is better to have a small number of close contacts than a wide circle. Avoid people who will give lip service to the idea of support and who do not commit or follow up. AVOID TOXICS and CYNICS at all Costs.

The five types of contacts

1 Those who will give you a job

2 Those who will give you the inside track on the job you are going for.
(They will be most useful to you when you are planning your answers to your questions.)

3 Those who will give you incidental information about the business, industry or job you are applying for

4 People with whom you will exchange information and support and have a productive reciprocal relationship

5 There is a fifth type of contact: The one who suggests you should call them sometime. They are often trying to impart the opposite message ("Don't you dare call me!"). It is also critically important to be realistic in your expectations from your contacts and to respect confidentiality by not passing on their details to third parties without their permission

> IMPORTANT! Show your appreciation for your contacts by thanking them, keeping the contact going and passing on anything that might be useful to them.

The three types of interviews:

1 **Practice interviews:**
Where you acquire the skills of talking to strangers and using a structuredinterviewprocess.Start by talking to people who have an interesting new hobby in the following way:

→ *Introduce yourself and indicate briefly your interest in finding out about the hobby, then ask how they became involved in it. Then ask about their likes and dislikes as well as looking for a few words of jargon and what they mean. Then, if you feel confident ask for any other names you could talk to. Thank them later by sending a text or an email*

2 **Career Research interviews:**
Where you are gathering information about a career or a specific job

→ *Approach your contact and use a structure like the following: After introducing yourself state your objective (e.g. gathering research on a possible career move) ask, as before, about likes and dislikes about the work, what the current challenges are in that business and how people cope. If you have time explore jargon words and look for relevant facts, figures and sources of information. At the end of the process ask for follow-on contacts — if you feel you have established proper rapport.*

If you are offered a job tell them that was not your purpose and politely decline — it may be a test of your probity. If they insist ask for time to think about it and come back to them later

❸ Job Interviews:
The subject of a book in itself. The interview is a structured conversation the objective of which is to establish if you have the skills, knowledge and attitudes which will ensure that you will be successful in the job. Most interviewees make the mistake of turning the interview into a hard sell for themselves

To be successful in the interview you need the following:

→ A clear idea of what the job you are looking for is about and whether you have what the organisation is looking for

→ To listen fully to questions and to what the interviewer says and to take your time in the process

→ To establish full, open and trusting rapport with the interviewers

→ To keep answers short and structured. Interviewers expect narrative answers to be in the form: What was the problem, what did you do and what was the result

→ A clear concise statement from you about who you are

in a professional sense: Your background, education, skills, professional interests, and future direction

→ A clear strategy as to deal with challenging issues or questions that may arise

→ A clear strategy as to how to handle the final question: "Anything you want to say to the board?"

If the job is really important to you:

→ Allocate up to 20 hours preparation

→ Research job in depth

→ Fine-tune your CV (résumé)

→ Rehearse structured questions

→ Use your supports to practice and refine your answers

→ Consider using a camcorder to practice your answers and to check how you come across

Making an impression

Here are some basic but effective techniques for networking:

Always carry a business card. Pay particular attention to the design and presentation of your business card — use a professional printer rather than doing it at home.

Use a spreadsheet or contacts programme on your PC to store numbers, emails and information about your contacts. Maintain regularly.

Exchange business cards. Take particular interest in the other person's business. After a productive meeting send an email or card noting a particular point which you found interesting.

Pass on information to your contact on the basis of needs they have identified to you. After you have done this a few times your contacts will be more inclined to return the favour.

Use a notebook to document meetings (it's the fastest way). You can enter the data on your computer later.

Send thank-you notes or a card where somebody has done you a favour.

Chapter 7 Summary

Detectives talk to everybody! You need contact to help you find the right job, the right information. However, you need good quality information at all stages – don't take what people say at face value.

❶ Everybody needs a network to support them, to provide feedback and information and to challenge suspect thinking

❷ It is vital to distinguish between different types of contacts and not to have unrealistic expectations

❸ Show appreciation and respect for your contacts

❹ Get used to talking to people to build up your confidence and experience in using structured interviews

❺ Spend at least 20 hours preparing for a job you are really interested in. The time will be taken up by research, tuning your application and preparing points for answers

Now prove it:

Activity 6

List some specific actions to make things happen.

	Action	Date	Desired outcome
1			
2			
3			

Other thoughts:

8

The Tool Kit

Chapter 8 outline
Resources to help you decide:

→ Listing and sifting
→ Journalling
→ Using the Internet
→ Managing your information
→ Prioritising
→ How do you make the future happen?
→ Meditation and Relaxation
→ Brainstorming
→ Incubating ideas

Introduction

Many people who examine their careers start from a position of having little clarity about what they want. This chapter contains some tools to help you identify, prioritise and visualise your future. Successful career change is a complex process that involves collecting information, sorting that information, identifying elements of your own career and moving forward through appropriate action on the basis of goals that you have set for yourself.

Listing and sifting

Listing is an essential first step in the career change process because you are not initially aware about all the information you need to know about yourself to make the right choices.

For a start it would be useful to list the following for yourself:

1 What success means to you (see Chapter 1)

2 What you really want/don't want from your career (see Chapter 2)

3 What you can do – your skills (see Chapter 3)

4 What subject you know something about and the fields of activity where they would be relevant (see Chapter 4)

5 What conditions are essential at work to ensure that you can perform at your very best. (see Chapter 5)

6 What your attitude and level of commitment to action is (see Chapter 6)

7 People who can support you and whom you can support in turn (see Chapter 7)

8 The major events and achievements in your life so far; there may be key things you have forgotten about

9 The failures and setbacks in your life- and what they taught you! This is the most challenging thing you can do – but also one of the most valuable

Why is listing so important?

Because we are not always immediately aware of our strengths and weaknesses.

Our brain conspires to hide our achievements from us so that, when we are stressed, all we think of is the negative information. We need <u>all</u> the information about ourselves to put our self-image in context. *(See also Chapter 3 in relation to Unconscious Competence etc.)*

Journalling

Writing up our most precious resource – our own life story

The most recent research on career development suggests

that our own story is one of the most important resources we have available to us, therefore it is essential that we understand our own life story and the lessons we have learned. There is a difference between **thinking** about our experiences and **writing** about them because meaningful action is a critical part of the process. In other words good thinking on its own is not sufficient for us to move forward we need to act, experiment, reflect and act again.

Activity 1

Consider writing a journal about your career and life changes over the course of the process. Be honest with yourself. Make it a warts and all account!

Take 10-15 minutes each day to log the following:

→ What happened in the last 24 hours/week that I am grateful for

→ What is really happening to me

→ How what is happening is impacting on the people around me

→ What I think should happen next

Julia Cameron (author of the Artist's Way) suggest writing spontaneously whatever comes to your mind. Over a period of weeks this can bring about significant personal change.

> *Why do I need this?*
> **Getting your story out there in print can help reduce your fear and increase your self-confidence.**

Using the Internet

The internet is a powerful resource for finding information. You can use the major search engines such as Google to find essential information about jobs or trends.

However, the internet suffers from two major limitations:

❶ Just because it is listed on the internet does not mean the information is true or complete

❷ Much material on the internet is out of date. Resist the temptation to trawl for jobs. Use the internet as a research tool to identify jobs that match your skills, expertise and personality. Before you apply for a job with a particular organisation do a complete background search on that organisation – consider non-internet sources such as your local library.

Managing your information

As you gather information you may become swamped with irrelevant material. To prevent this happening use the following process:

→ **Stage 1**
Collect Information

For example: Try to identify as many examples of your skills from work projects that you enjoyed. Include in your search *Special projects, Something that got you noticed or promoted*

Something that others commented on favourably. Be generous with yourself

→ **Stage 2**
Sift information

Sifting
Consider the items that you should exclude — because they are not relevant or essential to your career change process. For example, in listing your skills some very basic skills (such as talking or chatting) may be universal and best left out of the reckoning. Examine each piece of information you collect about yourself and ask the questions:

What is this piece of information telling me and how relevant is it to my career? Can I exclude it?

→ **Stage 3**
Organise your information

Organise your information into families. Try to work out the connections between the items and devise an overall structure e.g. if you are organising the subjects you are interested in consult textbooks to see how the subject is organised — this may give you ideas for job titles or fields of activity. Integrating the data produced in the job search and career search process is a seemingly difficult task that is made easy by the use of one page structures such as the Career Wallchart at the end of the book. Use fishbone diagrams and post-its to help you

→ **Stage 4**
Prioritise data within headings

Prioritise data according to relevance, importance etc. Your job is to make the data relevant, reliable and manageable. *Remember you will need both quantity and quality in your skills and expertise lists*

Prioritising

Career Development as a process works best when we have concentrated on the key objectives and the key issues. As well as knowing what is top of our lists, it is equally important to know the ranking of the top items. For example, you may have identified one particular skill as being your best one but what about the others? If you have the order of priority wrong it may point you in the wrong direction!

To help you ensure that the ranking of your key skills or areas of expertise is correct you should consider using the following priority grid.

There are four stages in prioritising:

❶ List, in *any* order, up to ten things you need prioritised. **(Section A)**

❷ Compare the items pair by pair. **(Section B)** When you compare the items put a circle around the number relating to the item that you prefer. In this way you will build up a picture of which items come out top. Do this for all the boxes which have pairs of numbers in them

❸ Count up the number of times each number was circled. Enter the scores in **Section C.** The items with the highest score have highest priority

❹ Rewrite the full list of items in their prioritised order **(Section D)**

> *Why do I need this?*
> **Instinctively you may know what your first choice is but prioritised lists help you make better decisions.**

How do you make the future happen?

By visioning it — using the data that you have accumulated through the various exercises.

You now know what skills you most prefer to use, what their objects are and how you work using these skills. Earlier (in

Meditation gives you a chance to stand back from your data and see the patterns between things.

Chapter 1) you identified your drivers — so you know what gives you satisfaction at work. Your ideas about fields in which you would prefer to be involved have become clearer — so have your ideal working colleagues, rewards and environment. As a career detective you have to combine these elements in a coherent picture. A well-tried and trusted method is by writing an account of a day in your future life when

The Priority Grid — *Your Own Personal League Table*

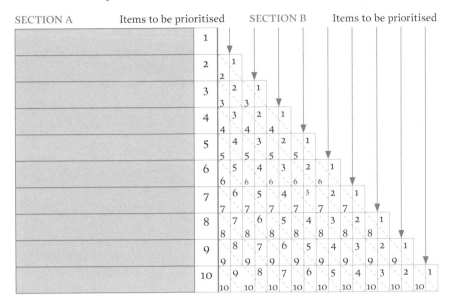

SECTION A   Items to be prioritised   SECTION B   Items to be prioritised

SECTION C

Count the rings!	1	2	3	4	5	6	7	8	9	10
How many times did you circle this number?										
Final Ranking/Placing (1st, 2nd, 3rd, etc)										

SECTION D

My Preferences — In order

1st	
2nd	
3rd	
4th	
5th	
6th	
7th	
8th	
9th	
10th	

these elements will be more part of your life than they are now.

As Somerset Maugham once said - *if you wish for the best* — you usually get it.

However, your vision should also be grounded in reality. Use both your left and right brain to make the vision as clear and as plausible as possible.

Take your time and enjoy your future.

Activity 2
Identifying your future Scenario

Write up a typical working day using the information from your wallchart:

→ *Skills, Interests, Working Conditions and Career Drivers. Articulate your vision as clearly as possible*

Start the story from the moment you wake; describe what you can see, hear and feel.

Fill in the rest (about 300-500 words at least are needed).

Work through the narrative until you get to the end of the day. What is your last thought at the end of the day?

Why do I need this?
Getting your story out there in print can help reduce your fear and increase your self-confidence.

Meditation and relaxation

There are many varieties of meditation ranging from very structured or "guided" mediation through to daydreaming. Meditation gives you a chance to stand back from your data and see the patterns between things. Meditation provides a place of stillness where the right side of the brain (the creative bit) can be let do its own particular work and help you integrate your data and help create your vision of the future. There are many schools of thought with regard to methods and objects of meditation. Choose one that suits your beliefs and ways of working.

Here are some options for meditations you could try later:

❶ Imagine a day in your life a year from now. What would it look like?

❷ Imagine yourself in a favourite spot in nature - what would you see, hear, smell, feel and taste?

❸ Try and empty your mind of conscious thoughts

④ Become present to your emotions for a few moments

⑤ Reflect on a mantra such as: What is the shape of the life to come?

Physical Relaxation

Physical relaxation is an important part of the process because it stimulates right-brain (creative thinking) – see the following chapter. Walking is one of the best ways of combining reflection and exercise.

Brainstorming

Brainstorming is useful to us to help us list key information without censorship. The main rules of brainstorming are:

① List everything

② Suspend judgment

③ Explore connections

④ Stay open to possibilities

⑤ Stay energised and focussed

Incubating Ideas

If you are stuck and problems seem insoluble – take a break into something completely different. Be kind to yourself if you get stuck - don't beat yourself up by labelling yourself as stupid. Accept that the brain needs time out to process your problem in the subconscious. The technique is similar to what we do in solving puzzles. Some people call it using the brains downtime!

The key is that you don't have direct access – but that doesn't stop you from using the resource as if you had.

Just go away and relax. Your dreams may even play back your problem to you in ridiculous ways – this is evidence that the incubating brain is working.

GREAT INCUBATORS in SCIENCE

1. Archimedes had his famous insight about the displacement of solids in liquid while sitting in his bath

2. The chemist Kekulé had a dream about six monkeys chasing each others tails. This dream allowed him to discover the ring structure of benzene and open a completely new field of industrial chemistry

On your return, your solution and maybe other ideas will have occurred to you.

Ask yourself the question: What would the solution to this problem look like, feel like?

Record your ideas (in writing) preferably and follow up later. Writing (rather than keyboarding on a computer) stimulates a wider range of brain cells than are used in pure thought.

Write it down, play with it, leave it, *and solve it!*

Chapter 8 Summary

A good detective reviews all the evidence, excludes the inessential, prioritises the visualises the possibilities.

Summary points from this chapter are:

1 List everything – but exclude trivial or non-essential material

2 Consider writing a journal to document your progress or learning

3 Prioritise the key items: Your skills, your expertise your ideal working conditions

4 Write a vision of your future based on the best information you have about yourself. Distinguish between a vision that is purely aspiration and one that builds on your unique gifts

5 Meditate and relax to get both mind and body into shape

6 Utilise the brains "downtime" to solve problems using your subconscious!

Activity 2

List some specific actions to make things happen.

Action	Date	Desired outcome
1		
2		
3		

WHEN things don't go to plan

9

Chapter outline
Some frequent challenges and problems

→ Family Issues

→ Peer groups

→ Career change as a form of bereavement - dealing with rejection

→ Special needs and so-called 'handicaps'

→ The need for tough thinking and straight talking

→ Ten common problems

→ The need for celebration and reward

Introduction

Life does not happen at our bidding;
we hit setbacks and become discouraged.
You may need to reflect and consider
what the real problems are and how
best to deal with them.

Selecting a correct career from the outset can be very difficult, if not downright impossible. At school we are asked to select subject for our final pre-college exams – on the assumption that we are clear as to what our future direction is. The fact that we are asked to do this right in the middle of puberty – which is itself turbulent – makes it all the more challenging. Add to this the expectations of family, peers and society in general and the odds against making the right choice first time become

When things get tough, prayer is not a substitute for hard work – it is part of it.

longer still. On top of that add the uncertainty of a volatile or poor economy and round it off with living in an uncongenial environment and the odds of

getting it right could well be zero. No wonder many people follow the herd or do what members of their family have done before and go for the safe bet! Before you start out on the intensive and extremely rewarding work of career and life planning you may need to do a check on yourself. Some factors may actually hold you back and may need to be attended to before the process can proceed.

Family

International research indicates that families play a strong role in determining the career choices we make – for both good and bad. However many career changers or job searchers – particularly teenagers – find themselves in the situation that where they cannot make up their minds as to which career path to take, they may be put in a position where their families may force the choice on them for the best of motives.

On the positive side: Following the career path pursued by other members of your family may be less risky than exploring new options – and will get a lot of support in doing this; but the danger is that it is their life you're living and not yours. As with peer groups, part of the work you may have to do is to separate from the family in terms of your job or career but not in terms of your kinship or belonging. This can be a very isolating process and one where you need to have other supports in place.

Changing your career may also involve change for others in your life

If you have been working in a job as a wage earner for others and you decide to change your job or career it follows that this change will affect the lives of the people closest to you. You may feel secure in changing your career but others who depend on you may have their own anxieties about their security, because your change in your status may affect them. Part of your work is to help your dependants and immediate family adjust. In a family situation this type of change may require consultation – or at the very least, informing others of your intentions ahead of time.

Peer Groups

Many processes assume that the individual is acting solely on their own initiatives. For some people, particularly teenagers and young adults the power of the peer group is very significant in determining their choices. Taking on a separate road from your peers may result in your isolation as the change in your own role actually may be an indirect challenge to the existence of the group. You may experience negative reactions or even rejection from your peer group. This challenge can be extremely painful but very developmental and may be another part of the maturation process. You may have disengaged from groups of people who are cynical and toxic in their approach. Your positive moves may be an inspiration to some but may be perceived as a threat by others!

Activity 1
If I change my career what impact will this have on others in my life?

Identify a number of significant other people in your life and the possible impact your change of career might have on them. What actions would be needed get them on-side?

How will this affect your thinking?

Example

Person	Impact	Actions
Example: Partner	Income may be affected; lifestyle will change. Social status may affected. May trigger fears regarding own security.	Support, listen to concern, consult and negotiate.

Why do I need this?
You are not the only one affected by your career plans.

People with special needs

Some people have special needs because of problems with vision, hearing or physical access to the workplace — they have their own special needs. If you are limited by the deficiencies in your bodies or in your mental state, how have you overcome the challenges of your situation in the past? How has your situation made you more aware and sharper to certain things than those around you? If you have a special need you may also have special gifts as well.

Bereavement, relationship problems and other emotional challenges

If you have recently suffered the loss of a loved one in your life through death, divorce or separation the process of recovery itself may interfere with the work of self -directed career change. The grieving process may take time to work through — and you should allow for this and not under-estimate the effort required. You may defer serious work on your career until you feel ready. This is an area where caution should be advised — you may wind up pushing yourself too hard and getting counter-productive results. Don't be afraid to seek support or professional help.

Career change as a form of bereavement - dealing with rejection:

The five stages of bereavement could well also apply to career change and subsequent rejection as you try to find a new direction. It is hard not to experience rejection very personally.

What is needed is an understanding of the following:

→ Rejection is universal — everybody gets rejected at some time or another
→ Most people don't share their own rejections with others
→ Many rejections (e.g. job applications) are made on the wrong grounds — you were the right candidate but they made the wrong call
→ There is a possibility you mis-judged the situation and that your rejection was justified - what you need is a clear sense of proportion and realistic expectations
→ Persistence combined with a healthy sense of realism is what ultimately wins the day

WANTED:
TOUGH CAREER COACH —
must be honest but tactful!

As well as unconditional supporters you may need a devil's advocate who will help make your thinking realistic and honest. If you are unwilling to do this career change may be a frustrating process!

The need for tough thinking and straight talking

If the process is getting tough there are a number of alternative approaches you could take — ranging from looking for gentle support, on one hand, to asking the most challenging questions of yourself (without falling into the trap of beating yourself up). The temptation is to blame too many of our difficulties on outside factors and to attribute blame to everything except ourselves. You may be partially or fully responsible for the situation you are in. To deal with these difficulties you may need a combination of support, good information and honest, incisive thinking — and that will require help. To make the process more effective — consider it as a reciprocal arrangement (which will empower both parties).

Ten common issues

Some positive choices you can make *and* Some hard questions to ask yourself!

What these issues have in common is that they are all statements which you could make about yourself. They all have an element of truth in them but they may be missing key elements of your situation – particularly that other people will not see your situation in the same way. The main problem is one of attitude – are you creating needless difficulties for yourself or are you articulating a problem that may not even exist?

Crunch time

Here are ten of the most common issues that hold people back with points a supporter and a tough career coach might make. Before you examine this list review Chapter 6 on attitude!

	What's your issue	What your supported would say	What your tough career coach might say
1	*"I can't get started: I am stuck"*	❶ Find somebody you can help and get them to support you! ❷ Review previous times you were stuck and how you re-started	❶ Are you really committed to moving forward? ❷ How badly do you need a change?
2	*"There are no jobs out there"*	❶ Review the national job statistics which show that even in recessions there are movements in and out of the workforce ❷ Target medium to small organisations in your area and find out how the employment patterns have changed over time	❶ How do you know that this is the case? ❷ Have you done enough research? ❸ To whom have you been talking?

3	"I can't make any decisions"	① Get into the habit of making small decisions – no matter how small every day ② Articulate and write down your fears	① Some of your concerns are real – get them into proper perspective ② What does it take to get you to make a real decision? Are you really committed?
4	"Nobody wants to talk to me"	① Find people who can pave the way for you. ② Change your method of approach. Look at the timing of your approaches	① Why? How can you make it easy for others to talk to you? ② What have you got that others might want?
5	"I am too old"	① Consider how your experience gives you the edge ② Identify your role models	① You're tired and others are getting that message. ② This is what your friends are saying isn't it? Why do you believe them?
6	"I am over-qualified; nobody will employ me"	① Be more selective in your job targets and in your presentations ② Change your point of approach to the organisation – use your contacts	① You may have given the impression that the job you applied for was beneath you! ② It's not just qualifications that get you the job – your skills set and your achievements are more important in the 21st century

7	*"I was fired/ laid off — no-one will want me"*	**1** Being laid-off is not the stigma it used to be — people change jobs more frequently these days **2** Others won't have a problem with this if you show what you learned from the experience	**1** Was this really a bolt from the blue? **2** How was your career going just before you got laid off? **3** Was your field in decline anyway? **4** Isn't it time for a change?
8	*"I am in recovery"*	**1** Find others in a similar recovery situation that you can team up with **2** Use your community **3** Study how others in recovery process have managed	**1** How well is your recovery process going? **2** Could you manage both at the same time? **3** This is a challenge which is worthy of you
9	*"I lack confidence"*	**1** You have not let this stand in your way in the past if you really wanted something badly enough **2** Count your blessings — and do it every day	**1** Do you think you are the only one? **2** What have you done to help others?
10	*"I am terminally shy"*	**1** Enrol a friend a partner to help you in the early stages **2** Thank people you make contact with during and after the process; they will respond!	**1** Who else do you know who is like you? **2** How do they manage their lives? **3** Is "shy" just another word for lazy? **4** What are you avoiding here?

Activity 2
What's holding you back?

This exercise is a tough one – to cut through the excuses that we make for ourselves and to ask the hard questions.

	What's your issue?	What your supporter would say	What your tough career coach might say
1		1 2 3	1 2 3
2		1 2 3	1 2 3

Why do I need this?
Two brains are better than one!

If all else fails: Consider this:

→ You have your health
→ You have access to clean water
→ You can worship the deity you believe in – or not.
→ You had enough to eat today
→ You have somewhere to sleep tonight
→ You live in a free world
→ You are not fearful about your physical survival
→ You have family and friends
→ You can speak freely in society
→ You have access to both public and private transport
→ You have access to some form of a pension plan.
→ Welcome to the top 1 % of people in the planet.

The need for celebration and reward.

It may seem in this chapter that a very hard road lies ahead. That could well be the case. However, because we are human we should recognise and celebrate our successes frequently and be thankful that we can move forward. Understand your own motivation and identify appropriate role models for yourself.

Chapter 9 Summary

Good detectives understand that life isn't easy. There are things like families, personal problems and special needs that make life more difficult for us than others and may give us an excuse for holding back.

1 Families play a major role in career choices, however there is the need to clarify your own path – but keep your proper place in the family

2 Peer groups may have an undue effect on your thinking – you make have to work on both your career and your peers!

3 If you are a person with special needs you have extra obstacles – but your limitations may give you a focus that others lack

4 Bereavement and other recovery processes may take priority over career change for a brief period

5 Recognise and celebrate your progress

Activity 3
List some specific actions to make things happen.

	Action	Date	Desired outcome
1			
2			
3			

WHEN and HOW will it come together?

10

Chapter 10 outline
Putting it together and making it happen?

→ Your Career = Your Chosen ROLE
   in Your Chosen FIELD
→ Phases of Career Development
→ Creating your future
→ Balancing Vision and Sustainability
→ Goal setting and you
→ Action plans

Introduction

This chapter draws together the information gathered in the previous ones. Once you are clear on what you are looking for and what have got to offer you can now proceed. To make your chosen career happen you have to commit yourself to a realistic course of action on the basis of the information you have gathered already. Revisit Chapter 5 where you identified possible roles and possible fields. If you are not clear on which is the best, use the priority grid in Chapter 8 to narrow the field down.

"I have learned that if one advances confidently in the direction of their dreams, and endeavours to live the life they have imagined, they will meet with success."
- Henry Thoreau

YOUR CAREER = Your chosen ROLE in your Chosen FIELD

Revisit the previous chapters to collect the major pieces of information relevant to the identification and successful management successful management of your career. Carefully examine your Career Blueprint before proceeding.

Finding your chosen role

Your chosen role can be deduced initially from your skill set (the WHAT).

Ask yourself the question: What jobs (roles) feature these skills?

You can also reduce the options by limiting them to your chosen fields.

Finding your chosen field

Your chosen field can be deduced initially from your expertise and interests (the WHERE).

Ask yourself the question: What fields/industries/disciplines use/value them?

You can also use your skills set to find the field of your choice. However, start by looking at your expertise and interests.

Activity 1

If you could make only one career choice what would it be?

Your chosen ROLE	Your chosen FIELD

Why do I need this?
Instinctively you may already know the one thing that is right for you.

TOTAL Career Choices = Optional Roles x Optional Fields

When you examine your skills set you may find that you have a number of alternative roles you could occupy (say 3) and a number of alternative fields you could work in (say 4).

TOTAL Career Choices = 3 Optional Roles x 4 Optional Fields = 12 Choices

If you consider all the possible combinations (12 in all) you have a range of options you could first prioritise (and evaluate) and then research. However, it may be more manageable to explore intermediate options in detail; instead of changing both role and field to consider keeping one. This can also give you the elements of a practical career path.

If you are considering transitioning from one career to another it is easier to change either the role or the field – but hardest to change both simultaneously.

Exploring the four types of career change:

You have four major options

Option	Role
1 **Stay in the same role and the same field**	The easiest option providing you are in the right role and the right field
2 **Keep the same role but move to a different field**	Easy to manage because your core job skills will remain the same
3 **Change your role but stay in the same field**	More difficult because you may have to change your skills set and develop new skills
4 **Change both role and field at the same time**	The most difficult option requiring the most change

Activity 2
List your optional moves

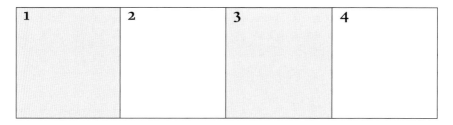

1	2	3	4

For example: You are a Systems Analyst (your role) in banking (your field) and you are considering a career as an instructor (chosen role) in a Education (your chosen field). Here are your options with a reality check!

Option	Role	Field	Reality Check
1	Systems Analyst	Banking	→ A lot of opportunity here —with your current employer and others — no major re-training needed. → **EASIEST OPTION – stay put!**
2	Systems Analyst	Education	→ Very specialised - you may need re-training. → **DIFFICULT – different challenges, different field**
3	Instructor	Banking	→ Can use your experience (inhouse training) – you may need new qualifications. → **MODERATELY DIFFICULT – same field but new role and new challenges**
4	Instructor	Education	→ Can use your experience (business schools) – you may need new qualifications → **MOST DIFFICULT – new challenges in new field. Green field situation!**

Activity 2 — *now try it yourself!*

Option	Role	Field	Reality Check
1			
2			
3			
4			

PHASES OF CAREER DEVELOPMENT

There are two major ways of looking at career development:

1 In a linear way — particular events happen at specific times of your life

2 The cyclical model — there is a continuing pattern of events

The linear model:
Phases of your career

The ages at which these changes occur are not the same for everybody but the general pattern has been well-validated by various researchers

→ **Young Adult (18-28): Establishment**
The main goal here is to leave home and establish your career. To do this you have to acquire expertise and essential skills

→ **The Thirties: Consolidation and re-evaluation**
Age thirty is a point at which many people feel the need to have established themselves in their career. It is a point at which we first get indications that time is moving on; up to then we may have regarded ourselves as immortal! The late thirties are typically a point where there is re-evaluation and a questioning of what has gone before but it can also be a period of consolidation, and a time to build a timetable for the future

→ **Middle Age (40-55): Crisis and Transition**
This period begins with the *Mid-life Transition*. This transition may come as early as the late 30s. It is a period when our perceptions become more important than our age. How a person feels about his or her life experiences are more significant than a chronological timetable indicating years of

life. With improvements in medical science and longevity 40 and 50 are not the end points that they were for a previous generation. There may be some very deep challenges during this period and the feeling may be that these challenges are unique to you. People in this stage have come to terms with life as stable personalities. It's a time for mental flexibility rather than rigidity. It's a time for emotional flexibility rather than emotional poverty

→ **Late Adulthood (55-75)**
Retirement becomes a real prospect at this stage. However, retirement in the 21st century is more likely to be a gradual withdrawal from the world of work than the sudden "cliff edge" retirements of the current or previous generations. Where a very dramatic and unplanned retirement occurs it has been found that a person may not physically survive the early years of a forced retirement. People in this band are called the young old (55 to 70 approximately) and the middle old (70 to 75 approximately)

→ **Old Age (Beyond 75)**
Probably the most challenging period with declining health in the last few years; the main difficulties are loss of contemporaries, friends and possibly a spouse. However, attitude and experience with dealing successfully with the earlier changes can make this a fulfilling one for us. Current age expectancies for men and women are 80 and 84 respectively. Start planning now!

2. The cyclical model

There are a number of recognized Phases in career development which are common to most

people. Research shows that Phases of career and life development are linked to particular ages in peoples' lives and there is a cycle of growth or turmoil, followed by a plateau of consolidation which is repeated several times in our working life. If we manage the turmoil at each of the Phases later transitions become relatively easier.

Activity 3
List times in your career where you think you were at any of the five stages above.

Ask the following questions:

→ *What were the turning points?*

→ *What did you learn?*

→ *What new skills have you acquired?*

→ *If you were to do it again what would you change?*

→ *What are the worries that proved groundless?*

→ *What are you most thankful for?*

Do you see any patterns?

Take as much time (and paper) as you need!

Check your Career Blueprint to check if your past career was giving you what you wanted and using your best skills and expertise.

> *Why do I need this?*
> **To find where you are at and how you can learn from past Success.**

Activity 4
Creating your future:

Go back to the scenario you did in Chapter 8.

→ Do you have a vision?

→ Is your vision sustainable? (Will it pay the bills? Do you have a secure future?)

> *Why do I need this?*
> **To bring a sense of reality into the process.**

Reality Check:
Balancing Vision and Sustainability

There are two extremes in visioning your future:

→ "Business as usual" – this assumes that nothing basically will change and you will remain in the same rut as before

→ "Blue skies" thinking – this assumes that anything is possible and that given the right conditions anybody can do anything

Your objective is to produce a vision that is somewhere between these two extremes – to make sure that you are not selling yourself short or overstating your situation. That is why you need a realistic inventory of your abilities.

The Macro Approach:

→ *Given the Phases outlined above draw a road map for yourself for your life to date and to age 80 (or so)*

→ *What have been the major milestones so far?*

→ *Where are you now?*

→ *What's your vision of what lies ahead?*

→ *At the end of it all – what would you like to look back on?*

The Micro approach:

→ Write a description of what a typical day would look like. Start the description from the moment you rise. Include all relevant material from the paragraphs above; describe the role you enjoy in the field of your choice. Try and achieve as realistic as possible

Activity 5
Evaluating your scenario

Your may find your left logical brain in conflict with the right creative brain (see Chapter 6). List some of the things that each side of the brain might be saying to you (I have given some typical examples).

The left brain will say: *Who do you think you are?* *You're past it!*	The right brain will say: *Go for it!* *Don't underestimate yourself.*

Ask yourself these questions

Which voice sounds most like you? Which one would you rather be listening to for the rest of your life? What obstacles do you have to tackle to move forward?

> **Why do I need this?**
> **If you do not constantly refresh your vision it will disappear! If you continually listen to the negative voices your vision will not materialise.**

Looking for a job or a career?

Make sure that you are aiming for a career and not a job! (See Chapter 1)

❶ Make sure that the job you apply for is one that matches your qualifications, interests, skills and values and has a place in your long-term plan

❷ Research on successful candidates in selection processes says that your likelihood of success will be greatly improved by doing background research on the company you are interested in and on the methods of selection that they use

❸ In filling a job vacancy employers are looking for someone to help them solve their problems and advance their business. Your job is to help the employer match you to the job

❹ Successful job-hunters do not rely on one method exclusively – such as the internet or advertisements in papers and journals. Research suggests that your rate of success is increased if you use a small number of different methods – at best no more than four

GOAL SETTING and YOU

Much has been written about achieving goals using a SMART format.

S = Specific
M = Measurable
A = Achievable
R = Relevant
T = Time-bound

The translation of complex values into goals is a difficult and challenging one requiring self-knowledge and sound judgement.

It might be time to redefine the smart goals as follows:

121

Ⓢ **= Specific and Stretching**
These goals will use **your** full potential

Ⓜ **= Made to Measure**
For **you**

Ⓐ **= Artistic – creative**
Will allow you flexibility

Ⓡ **= Realistic**
For **your** capacities

Ⓣ **= Time-bound**
But not threatening

Nothing will happen unless you set, monitor and achieve your goals on a continuous basis.

CREATING an ACTION PLAN

"The journey of a thousand miles begins with but a single step." (Confucius)

If you fail to set goals you will not move very far: *"Failing to Plan means Planning to Fail."*

ZERO PLUS ONE GOAL SETTING

Setting goals is a common self-management technique which can frequently lead to frustration as the goals can be over-stated and you are set up for constant failure. "Zero plus one" goal setting is a way to go forward on the basis

of setting small, immediately-achievable goals. For example you could set yourself the objective of losing 10 kilos bodyweight this month

→ Could you achieve it?

→ How about achieving 1 Kilo in a month?

→ If that is manageable and you achieve your objective what is the next objective you will set yourself? One kilo next month – or would you go two?

That is what we mean by Zero Plus One Goal setting.

The Zero Plus One technique identifies the smallest unit that you can work with that will convince you that you have some small measure of control over your problem.

Try setting yourself some Zero Plus One goals for your career or job search:

For example:

→ *Next week I shall write up and analyse one skills story*

→ *The following week I shall write up two*

→ *The week after I shall write up two and make notes for a third etc*

FAIL to PLAN and you are PLANNING to FAIL!

Career Planning and looking for a job.

If your focus is on looking for a job you need to prepare yourself by assessing the opportunities on the basis of the information on your Career Blueprint. If they meet your criteria you can now proceed to apply for a job confident that you will be able to make a serious mid-to-long term commitment to your prospective employer. Now you are ready to make the approach.

Varieties of Goal-Setting

The challenge in goal-setting is that you need to be constantly setting different types of goals - short, medium and long-term. Documenting and reviewing goals is a good way to keep yourself motivated. Ensure that you reward yourself for achieving intermediate goals.

"Celebration is an integral part of the achievement process- Don't leave it out!"
Kevin O'Kelly, *Author*

The best and worst ways to approach employers

A summary of the most and least effective strategies in getting a job:

Least effective	Most effective
→ Sending unsolicited applications and CVs	→ Discovering the "hidden" job market through focussed networking
→ Answering ads in newspapers and journals	→ Approaching employers following
→ Using only one method	→ In-depth research
→ Some job-finding agencies	→ Targeting small to medium-sized businesses
→ "Winging it!"	→ Using your networks properly
	→ Having a number of alternatives

Application and Screening Processes and How to deal with them.

There are many selection processes in use in contemporary organisations. Here are the more usual ones.

Process	Strategy
Application form	Be sure to match your skills and expertise to the requirements of the job. The screening rate may be as low as 10%. What will put you in the top 10% - on paper?
Curriculum Vitae	Beware sending in unsolicited CVs — companies regard them in the same way as spam on your PC. Send in your CV when asked for it. Match the content of the CV to the business to which you are applying
Ability and Personality Tests	Ability tests are useful to establish what percentile of the population you belong in. They cover verbal and numerical reasoning. There are specialised tests to check your ability to programme computers or to handle office tasks. Doing practice tests will help — but use good up-to-date sources
Presentations	Companies are using these more often nowadays because they are seen as a good predictor of how you will fit into company culture. In this technique good preparation will really pay off
Selection Interviews – Including Competency-based Interviews.	Interviews nowadays tend to be very structured. In competency-based interviewing the structure of the interview is based on the behaviour of an effective performer — therefore it is important that you do your research about the business and the type of work you will be asked to do
Telephone Screening	A short interview on the phone. Designed to be short and very clear cut. Prepare by practising short answers and focussing on what makes you suitable for the company or the job you are applying for
Assessment Centres	A process which combines elements of the above – including interviews, presentations and "what if" scenarios. You may be asked to make a short sales presentation or deal with a member of staff with a work or attitude problem
Peer Assessment	You are assessed by your future colleagues — to see if you will fit in with the culture of the company and perform to the levels expected in realistic work conditions

Summary Chapter 10

As a career detective you now
all the information you need to
achieve success.

Your last checklist

❶ Make a realistic inventory of
what you need, what you know
and the skills you possess to
achieve your goals

❷ Your ideal career is a
combination of the ROLE you
are best suited to in the FIELD
of activity that uses your
favourite areas of expertise

❸ Every career has its landmarks;
mid-career crises are a part
of living

❹ Visualise your future career
judiciously balancing your
aspirations with a realistic
picture of yourself

❺ Be strategic in the way that
you identify opportunities and
approach potential employers

❻ Set goals – small, medium and
large; achieve them and don't
forget to celebrate!

YOUR CAREER BLUEPRINT	Chapter 10 MY CAREER = MY chosen ROLE(S) and FIELD(S)		
Enter into the boxes all the results of the featured activities in the Chapters as numbered here			

1. WHY? Chapter 1 Your success statement	In my career I would like the following Outcomes, Rewards, Values, Drivers, Life style		

2. WHAT? Chapter 3 List here: Your transferable **SKILLS** Their **OBJECTS** (what you use the skills with) and favourite **TRAITS**	**FAVOURITE SKILLS**	**OBJECTS**	**TRAITS**
	1. 2. 3. 4. 5.	1. 2. 3. 4. 5.	1. 2. 3. 4. 5.

3. WHAT? Chapter 3/4/5 **WHERE?** List here: Favourite **SUBJECTS** Favourite **FIELDS** of activity include possible **ROLES**	**Favourite SUBJECTS**	**Possible ROLES**	**Possible FIELDS OF ACTIVITY**
	1. 2. 3. 4. 5.	1. 2. 3. 4. 5.	1. 2. 3. 4. 5.
Best working conditions for me would need to include these:	1. 2. 3. 4.		

4. HOW? Chapter 6 Describe here your: Attitude Behaviour Level of Commitment	Attitude: Behaviour: Commitment:		

5. WHO? Chapter 7 List here key people in your life: Your networks, Contacts, Dependants and People you support	**NAME**		**ROLE**

6. WHEN? Chapter 10 **HOW?** List Here: Your short and Long-term Goals (be Super SMART!)	**Short-Term GOALS**		**Long-Term GOALS**
	1. 2. 3. 4.		1. 2. 3. 4.